# WYRLEY & ESSINGTON CANAL

## THROUGH TIME

Ray Shill

AMBERLEY PUBLISHING

First published 2013

Amberley Publishing
The Hill, Stroud
Gloucestershire, GL5 4EP

www.amberley-books.com

Copyright © Ray Shill, 2013

The right of Ray Shill to be identified as the
Author of this work has been asserted in accordance
with the Copyrights, Designs and Patents Act 1988.

ISBN 978 1 4456 1063 4

British Library Cataloguing in Publication Data.
A catalogue record for this book is available from
the British Library.

Typeset in 9.5pt on 12pt Celeste.
Typesetting by Amberley Publishing.
Printed in the UK.

# Contents

# Introduction

The Wyrley & Essington was conceived as an independent canal for the carriage of coal from collieries at Essington and Wyrley Bank to Wolverhampton, and with a branch to Birchills, to carry coal for the use in Walsall. It was seen as an important supply and one that would compete with the mines at Bilston, Coseley and Tipton, which were served by the Birmingham Canal Navigations (BCN). The original route to Essington was granted in an Act of Parliament in 1792, with construction starting that year. As work proceeded in making the canal, a second Extension Act was applied for and granted in 1794, which gave powers to extend the canal from the Birchills Branch to Coventry Canal at Huddlesford, serving the mines at Goscote and Brownhills, as well as a branch to serve limestone quarries at Hay Head and Rushall.

Building the extension was associated with more extensive engineering, including a deep cutting at Catshill, an embankment near Pipe Hill and thirty locks to take the canal down to the level of the Coventry Canal.

The first part to be opened was the original route to Essington and the five locks that raised the level of the canal to the Essington Wood Mines. Another five locks were required for a branch canal to Essington 'New' Colliery, the highest point on the Wyrley & Essington Canal, and the West Midlands canal network. The main line to Huddlesford was next completed and this work was followed by the branches to Lords Hayes and Hay Head (Daw End).

Water supply was obtained from a few streams that were diverted into the canal and a reservoir at Sneyd. Another projected reservoir at Catshill was abandoned in favour of one on Cannock Chase. This second reservoir became an important supply of water to the canal. All construction of the branches and the Cannock Chase Reservoir feeder was completed by 1801.

Trade on the Wyrley & Essington did not achieve its full potential, but it proved a useful supply of water for the adjacent navigations. Coal mines and early ironworks alongside the Wyrley & Essington had mixed fortunes during this period, including some closures. Trade along the waterway improved after 1840, following the merger of this canal with the Birmingham Canal Navigations. Three new link canals were made to facilitate trade between the two waterways. Trade, particularly the coal trade, was massively increased following the development of new collieries across the Cannock Chase Coalfield. It was to sustain traffic along the waterway through the days of Birmingham Canal Navigations' ownership to the public ownership of the docks and inland waterways executive, only effectively ceasing with closure of the mines during the 1960s.

**Map of the Birmingham Canal Navigations Network, 1913**

The complete Birmingham Canal Navigations network comprised five elements: Birmingham Canal; Birmingham & Fazeley Canal; Wyrley & Essington Canal; Dudley Canal; and new-build waterways that included the Bentley, Cannock Chase Extension, Rushall and Tame Valley canals.

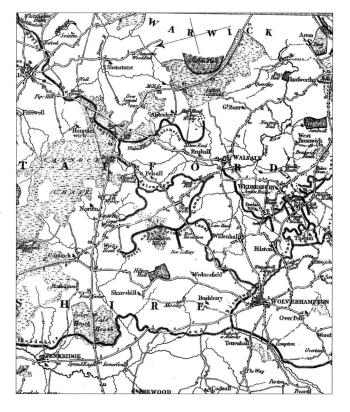

**Carey's Map of the Canal Network**

Carey showed the canals as per parliamentary schemes and surveys, but not necessarily built. In this section the Wyrley & Essington Canal is shown from top (Huddlesford) to bottom (Horsleyfields Junction BCN). The section to Lords Hayes (Lords Hay according to Carey) was not built in this form, nor was the canal to Wyrley Bank completed until 1858!

5

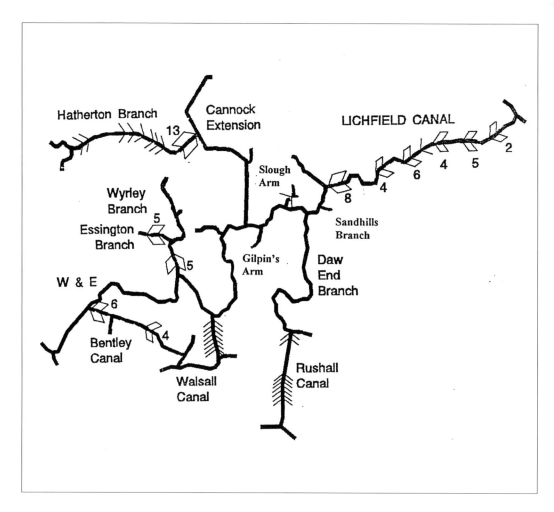

**Wyrley & Essington Canal Main Line, Branches and Connections**
Above is a map of the Wyrley & Essington Canal main line, branches and connections.

Chapter One

# Building the Canal

The Wyrley & Essington Canal was promoted during 1791 and 1792, leading to Parliament granting permission for the venture in April 1792. It was one of many such canals that were to be authorised and built during this period. So great were the numbers of new waterways contemplated that this time is sometimes referred to as 'Canal Mania'.

Those keen to promote any venture needed to gather enough funds together to finance the completion of the project. For canals, as with many other contemporary civil undertakings, a share issue provided the necessary funds to form a joint-stock company, which ran the affairs of the canal. Those who purchased shares did so in the hope of receiving a reasonable return on their money. There had to be some guarantee of success, therefore, to attract the necessary capital.

The aim of the Wyrley & Essington Canal was to link existing coal mines at Essington with the towns of Walsall and Wolverhampton. When the idea was first formulated, the nearest navigable waterway was the Birmingham & Fazeley Canal, which had been initially built for similar reasons, that is the transport of coal from the Bilston collieries to Birmingham.

It seems likely that the prime movers behind the Wyrley & Essington scheme were James Hordern and Henry Vernon. Vernon was the owner of the mines at Essington, while Hordern was a Wolverhampton banker. Vernon's mines were on the Bloxwich side of Essington and carriage of the coals was only possible by road. The turnpike from Walsall to Churchbridge, through Bloxwich, passed close to these mines and there were also roads of good quality (coal roads), which existed at the time of the Essington enclosure. Despite these resources, the market for Vernon's coal was limited. Transport charges added to the cost of coals raised at the pithead. Coal could be taken to towns such as Walsall and Wolverhampton, but the coal transhipped into boats at places like Calf Heath (Staffordshire & Worcestershire Canal) and Wolverhampton would have to compete with the cheaper coals mined closer to the waterway. The solution was to bring the waterway to the mines and make them profitable. As the idea gathered momentum, it would have been realised that the canal would serve other interests and possibly other mines yet to be opened.

The original intention of the promoters was to build a canal from the main line of the Birmingham in order that the products of the collieries at Wyrley & Essington could be brought to the towns of Wolverhampton and Walsall; and to render the conveyance of coal, corn, ironstone, limestone and other produce less expensive. The Act of 1792 provided for a level line from Horseley Fields Junction near Wolverhampton to Sneyd Junction, near Bloxwich, where one branch was to run up five locks at Sneyd to Wyrley Bank (with a branch up five locks to a colliery at Essington), and another to Birchills near Walsall. Shorter branches were also to be authorised at Ashmore Park.

A degree of organisation was required to gather finance and get a bill through Parliament. It seems that, in the case of the Wyrley & Essington line, a small and select band did the initial planning. Those involved were chiefly based in and around Wolverhampton. Hordern had his bank there; the solicitors Chrees & Wightwick were also based there. They helped to arrange for the Act to pass through Parliament. William Pitt also lived locally. He was employed to survey the best route. Other associates included Major Walter Haynes and John Bishton, an ironmaster from Shropshire. William Pitt had completed his initial survey by August 1791, when an advertisement was published in the local papers making the announcement for the intended canal.

The task of getting the Bill through Parliament was often complicated by opposition from other canal companies, who feared fresh competition; or landowners, who might object to the canal passing through their property. The Wyrley & Essington route promised to bring traffic onto the Birmingham Canal and their proprietor's intentions, as published, were not to compete with the trade on the Birmingham Canal. Perhaps the only questionable intention, at this point, as far as the BCN was concerned, would be the branch to Walsall, where the Birmingham Canal Company also had designs to serve. The managing committee of the Birmingham Canal decided to ask the proprietors' views at a special meeting held on 10 February 1792.

There was no opposition to the Wyrley Canal Bill, although the Conduit Lands Trust had to be recompensed before the Bill was presented to Parliament. The Wyrley & Essington Bill passed through Parliament and received Royal Assent on 25 April 1792. Having gained Parliamentary approval, the meetings commenced to be recorded in a book of proprietors' minutes. The first meeting of proprietors is recorded as taking place on 10 May 1792.

The Act provided for a canal from Wyrley Bank to Wolverhampton, where a junction was to be made with the Birmingham Canal at Horseley Fields. Branches were to be made from Sneyd to Birchills near Walsall and also to Ashmore Park and Pool Hayes, where mines were being developed. A stop lock was to be provided at the junction and all boats passing from or to the Birmingham Canal would be subject to a payment of toll to the Birmingham Company.

William Pitt was appointed engineer to the Wyrley & Essington Canal, but his role is better described as surveyor. Pitt had already built up a reputation as a very competent surveyor and it is in the planning of the route of the canal that he was chiefly involved. The task of building the waterway fell to Wolverhampton engineer John Brawn. The Brawn family were stonemasons, based at Wolverhampton, and Samuel together with his sons were paid by the Staffordshire & Worcestershire Canal Company for work that assisted building that waterway in 1766–72.

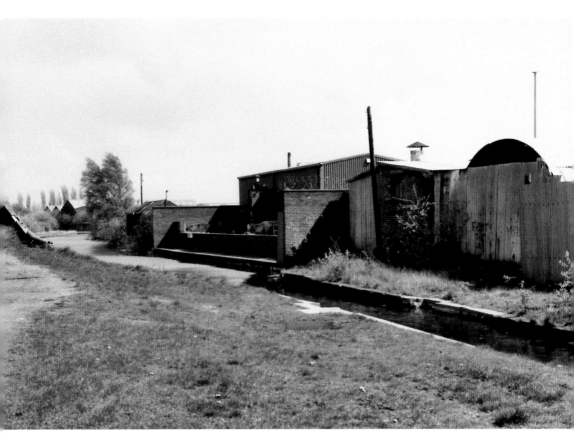

**Horseley Fields Stop, Wolverhampton**

The start of the Wyrley & Essington Canal was the stop where there were initially four sets of gates. During this time the Wyrley maintained an independent existence; the junction with the Birmingham Canal Navigations was made with a small difference (about 6 inches) in level, with the higher level on the side of the Wyrley Canal. This ensured that water was not lost to the Wyrley from the Birmingham. But if the level on the Wyrley side should drop, the second set of gates were brought into use either to restrict traffic or measure what water did pass through to Wednesfield. There was an overflow weir on the far side of the lock and this functioned as such through to 1846. For some six years after the merger of the two systems, the higher level was maintained as the Wednesfield Level by the BCN and then abandoned. This event was accompanied by a similar change at Sneyd, and this act ensured a lock-free section between Wolverhampton and the developing new coalfield on Cannock Chase.

# The Original Wyrley
# & Essington Canal

Any canal venture required sufficient finance to enable its success. Construction and land-purchase was an expensive outlay that had to be found in a relatively short period of time. Once constructed and opened to traffic, tolls and rents would provide revenue, which hopefully would pay for maintenance, improvements, rates or tithes, shareholders' dividends and staff wages.

The problems of canal finance were manifold. Some concerns found it necessary to have additional share issues in order to complete their waterway. Other schemes were never finished due to inadequate funds. In the case of the Wyrley & Essington Canal, the matter of finance was addressed before the Act was obtained. The notice published on 6 August 1791 asked for funds and it would appear that those funds became available in sufficient amounts for those behind the venture to proceed. In effect, a group of proprietors were formed before the Act. Nothing, to date, has been traced about the activities of this group, but it would seem likely that the attorneys Chrees & Wightwick would have recorded their affairs.

The role of solicitors and attorneys in canal and railway affairs is perhaps one which has been neglected by researchers. Yet they were integral to the running of the concern. The solicitors' firm frequently provided a member to fill the role of secretary to the transport company. In the case of the Wyrley & Essington Canal, it was Thomas Devey Whitwick who was to become their first secretary. William Chrees, junior, later replaced him, and later still, John Simpson Rutter, another attorney, filled this post.

Knowledge of legal procedure was important to prepare the wording of the Act, arrange share issues and to deal with the mountains of paperwork generated by the process. Knowledge of financial matters was also important and James Horden, who became treasurer for the canal company, was a banker and accustomed to financial dealings.

Those who subscribed to the Wyrley scheme became the proprietors for the proposed canal. In April 1792 they were asked to attend a meeting at the Swan Inn, Wolverhampton, 'on particular business'. This would have been their last meeting before that first Act received Royal Assent and the 'new' Wyrley & Essington Canal Company was formed.

The first Act enabled the Wyrley & Essington Canal Company to raise £25,000 in shares of £125 each, with authorisation to raise another £20,000 on each of those shares if required, and a further £20,000 by mortgage. Their first meeting recorded in the proprietors' minutes took place at the Red Lion Inn, Wolverhampton, on 10 May 1792.

Calls on the share issue were made by the clerk and published in the local newspapers. Amounts, usually £10 at a time, were collected at different dates and, as required, until the full value of the share was received. This was a standard process adopted by most canal companies.

Once the 'new' Wyrley Company had been formed, a committee to run the affairs of the canal was appointed. The second meeting of proprietors held at the Red Lion, 10 November 1792, confirmed that this committee would comprise four people: the Revd William Lawson, Walter Haynes, James Hordern and Henry Eld. Later on other people, including William Beto Taylor and Henry Villiers, would also serve on the committee.

John Brawn entered into a formal contract to build the Wyrley & Essington Canal. He was to be paid so much for cutting and making the waterway complete. Payment was broken down into the type of work done and some of it was distance-related. The physical work of cutting the channel was charged by length, but where embankments or cuttings were needed an extra payment was needed. There were payments for making the towpath, making fences and setting the quick (a hawthorn hedge). Where locks and bridges were required, bricks were made and stone cut.

The infrastructure along the line of the Wyrley & Essington Canal was made from bricks, stone and wood. The bricks were made from local clays in temporary kilns and taken to the site. Experienced brickmakers would be employed for this task. The job of bricklaying would also be assigned to skilled men. Stone was brought to the works and shaped by stonemasons to form coping stones for locks and bridges, stop-plank grooves, quoins and sills for lock gates. Carpenters were also required to make lock gates, bridges and other types of woodwork.

As the work progressed, the contractors would be subject to inspection to ensure that the work was done competently. The cutting undertaken by John Brawn was frequently along level ground. One notable exception was the Wednesfield embankment that lay between Horseley Fields and New Cross. At a committee meeting held at Major Hayne's in October 1792, Brawn announced 'the embankment w'od be turned in two months from this day without any increase in men, the number is thirty, the remainder of the line to the collieries by 24th June next excepting locks and brickwork'. The lock work comprised five at Sneyd and another flight of five locks were needed to raise the canal up to the upper-summit level, which served Essington Wood Colliery.

The actual period of construction proved to be longer than Brawn's confident hopes, yet he proceeded well to start with. By November, Haynes reported that a brickmaker, Michael Hadley of Dudley, had been appointed to throw up clay and make bricks at Wednesfield. Work on the embankment had been delayed as Mr Brawn was waiting to get his carpenter out of Hampshire. It seems that Brawn was engaged on another contract where some of his key men were employed. Canal contractors frequently had a hard core of loyal employees who followed them from contract to contract.

Michael Hadley was to go to Mr Lane's land to make the bricks, and then proceed to Bentley Hay to make 600,000 bricks there. Mr Brawn's brickmaker from Hampshire, Hardman, was expected by Christmas to make 800,000 bricks between Sneyd and Essington Wood. The task of building the locks and bridges was given to the bricklayers, who worked together as a set of three. These bricks would all be handmade. In places where a brick bridge was not needed, a wooden swing bridge would be provided. Clay would be thrown up and left to weather during the winter for brickmaking to commence the following April. A quantity of bricks had already been made for Brawn. The number was sufficient to complete four bridges at the Wolverhampton end.

The stone for coping and lock purposes was obtained as required. Mr Fereday was stated to have supplied some stone for the stop lock, while other stone was purchased from the quarries at Tixall (near the Staffordshire & Worcestershire Canal). By November 1792, 100 men were employed on the contract, with 25 assigned to the Wednesfield embankment. Brawn had promised Haynes 'to stir no man from the embankment till finished'.

The task of acquiring land lay with Mr Pitt and the solicitors. Pitt had to set out the route and detail all the landowners. A price was then agreed for the land taken for the use of the canal company. If a price could not be agreed then commissioners would be appointed to decide the value. Normally two commissioners would decide the amount, but if they could agree a third would be called to give a final judgement. The commissioners called upon for this service included John Bishton, who acted on behalf of the company.

As work progressed, Brawn suggested alterations to the route at Pool Hayes. After consultation with William Pitt, a shorter, and straight, section was added to the plan-book. The Act of Parliament had authorised two short canal branches to serve coal mines in this area, but there is no evidence to suggest either were built. Tram roads were made instead to bring coal down to the canal side from the collieries, which developed around Pool Hayes. By January 1793, water had been let into part of the canal to enable Brawn to move soil by boat. John Brawn asked for additional payment for this traffic, but was informed by the committee that it was included as part of the contract.

The Act of Parliament specifically states that a navigable canal was to be made 'from, or from near, Wyrley Bank', where coal mines existed. Yet the canal never reached this place at this time, but terminated short, near the Essington Wood Old Colliery belonging to Henry Vernon. Vernon had begun a new mine on the west side of Essington Wood. During February 1793, plans were made to build the collateral canal from Whitmore's Meadow to the intended new engine accommodating Vernon's mines. This is the first mention of the branch canal that became known as the Essington Canal. This branch was probably constructed between 1793 and 1794, and comprised a rise of five locks.

Work on the main line was delayed, especially in the Bloxwich area where the canal had to be taken around the hillside. Today there is little evidence of a hill there, but subsequent mining operations have altered ground levels. When William Pitt surveyed this area, he clearly thought that it was important to adopt the route to which the canal was finally built. It may be that the plan was altered at the point. By February 1793, John Brawn had doubts whether he would finish the canal to Walsall in time due to additional mileage caused through passing around Bloxwich Hill.

The number of men employed on the works now numbered between 100 and 120. By March 1793, Brawn had commenced to throw up clay for the Walsall Branch. A Mr Higgins was requested to come over for this work. Concern was felt among the members of the committee that men were leaving the works for other canal contracts. The men were paid 3 shillings a day by Brawn, but the committee suggested an inducement of a free dinner on Easter Monday plus one shilling worth of ale, and that every man who did not leave work should have another one shilling worth of ale on every first Monday of the month.

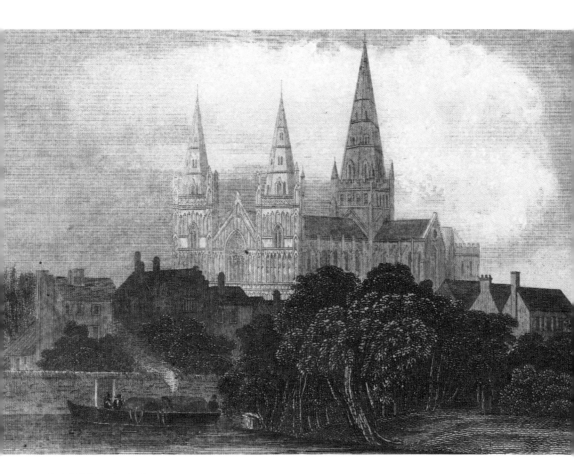

**Lichfield Cathedral**
Lichfield Cathedral and the town of Lichfield, with a canal boat depicted in foreground. The 'narrowboat' is represented with cloths covering part of the hold. The cabin is shown with smoke rising from a stove on board. The lack of a towpath is to be noted as the canal passed to the south of Lichfield, descending from Lock 19 through to Lock 22. If it was from this perspective the towpath would have been on the right.

# Features of the Original Canal
## Wolverhampton–Sneyd–Birchills

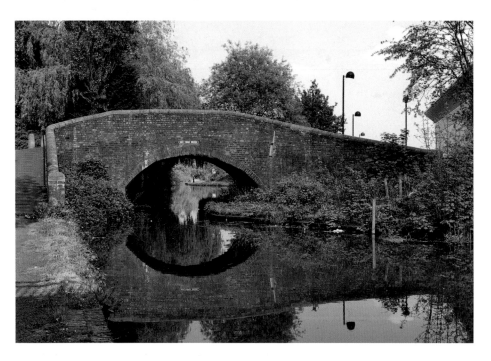

**New Cross Bridge, 2011**
The bridge over the canal at New Cross is a survivor from the early time of the Wyrley & Essington Canal. The black and white image captures an ice-bound scene and shows New Cross Bridge, the junction with the Bentley Canal and the Toll Office at the junction. (*Below photograph: Colin Such*)

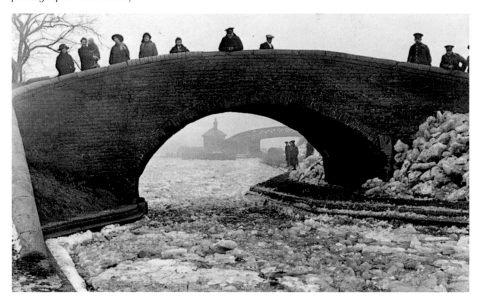

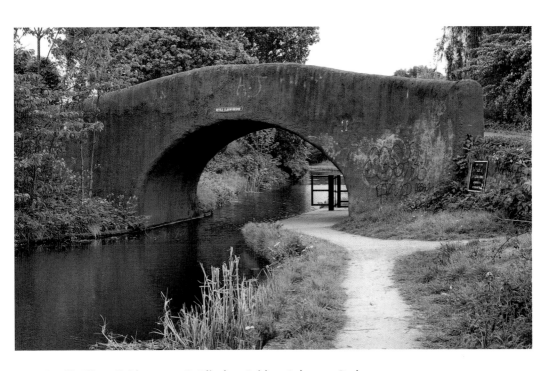

**Devil's Elbow Bridge, 2011 & Olinthus Bridge, Ashmore Park**
The canal east of Wednesfield had a sharp turn, and this feature led to the bridge there being named 'Devil's Elbow'. This is an old bridge, built during the early period of the canal, and has survived in this form as it carries a minor road over the waterway. The bridge carried the road to Ashmore Park over the canal. Beyond this bridge was a basin and terminus of a tramway from the Ashmore Park collieries.

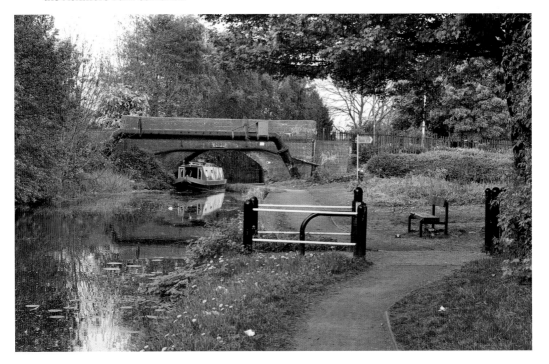

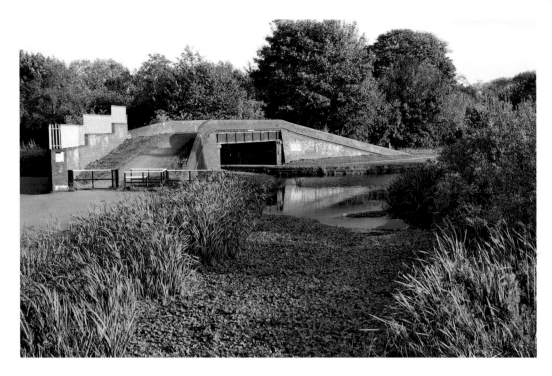

**Sneyd Junction, 2011 & Bottom Lock, Sneyd Locks**

The original route of the main line to Essington lay along the weed-covered canal in the bottom-centre of the canal, with the intended branch to Birchills on the left. Once the extension canal through Brownhills to Lichfield and Huddlesford passed through Parliament, the Birchills route became the main line. Of the five locks that comprise the Sneyd flight, only the bottom lock remains exposed, offering a target for graffiti and vandals.

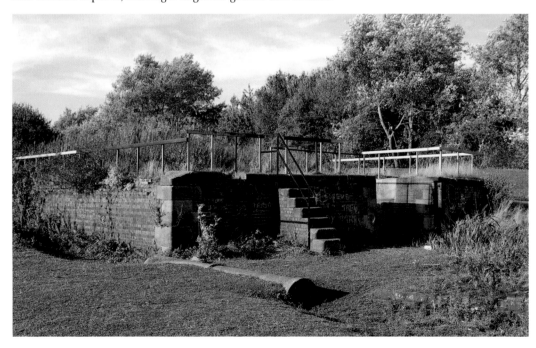

# Wyrley & Essington
# Extension Canal

Plans for the Wyrley & Essington Extension Canal from Birchills to Huddlesford were formulated during 1793 and proposals for the second Act, based on plans surveyed by William Pitt, were discussed at a committee meeting held in July. William Chrees Junior was sent out to Derby, Nottingham, Ludlow and Gloucester to procure land for the extension.

In January 1794, representatives from the Birmingham & Fazeley Canal and the Staffordshire & Worcestershire Canal met people from the Wyrley Company at Dudley to discuss the proposed Extension Bill.

Both companies were clearly concerned about the competition created by the new through route to the Coventry Canal. Following this meeting, John Houghton, for the Birmingham Canal, requested that a clause be put into the Bill imposing a duty of 3*d* per ton on all coal that may be carried out of the Birmingham Canal along the Wyrley Canal to Fazeley, in addition to the duty presently payable thereon.

The Extension Act received Royal Assent in March 1794. This act empowered the raising of 600 shares of £125 each, which comprised 400 new shares and 200 'free' shares allotted to the existing shareholders. This benevolent 'gift' may be explained by the fact that the £125 shares' owners, of the 1792 Act, had contributed, or were about to contribute, towards the additional £20,000 authorised by the first Act. If this were the case then £45,000 would have been raised for a 'paper' value of £50,000. The original shareholders would therefore benefit by paying the equivalent of £112.50 for each share of their total share allocation, instead of the £125.00 face-value.

William Pitt was entrusted with surveying the new route, including branches to the limestone mines at Hay Head via Rushall and Lords Hayes quarries. The new plans involved incorporating most of the Walsall Branch, from Sneyd to Birchills, then under construction, into the main line of the canal through to Huddlesford. From Birchills the canal turned northwards through Coalpool and Goscote to Pelsall, where there were collieries. The line was the continued to Brownhills, close to P. Hussey's coal works, and then by Catshill, Ogley, Muckley Corner and Lichfield.

Despite assurances from John Brawn, the construction works on the original line dragged on through the winter of 1793 and into 1794. In March 1794, Parliament authorised the Wyrley & Essington Extension Canal Act. This new project was of a more substantial nature. There were proposals for a deep cutting at Catshill and a flight of locks to bring the canal down to the level of the Coventry Canal at Huddlesford. An advertisement was inserted in *Aris's Gazette* for canal-cutters on the Wyrley & Essington Extension to make the canal on Cannock Heath. The first to apply was a Mr Carne, who submitted quotes for the Catshill 'deep cutting'. Carnes had devised a mechanical cutting machine and planned to use it on this contract. His prices were relatively high and a cheaper price was quoted by George Miles, who appears to have been given the work. The bulk of the other work was given to John Brawn.

The line from Ogley to Huddlesford required a number of locks. Willliam Pitt gave the rough location of these locks by the indication of a dotted line. The canal that was built differed somewhat from what was originally proposed. Pitt, conscious of water supply, conceived a lock that would conserve water in segments of a semi-circular side pound. Elsewhere the intermediate lock pounds were extended through side pounding, where space was available that

Mr Jones of Fordhouses was given to contract, to fence the canal from the Bloxwich–Bentley Road Bridge as far as Catshill. This job included the provision of wicket gates on the towpath.

Meanwhile, preparations were being made to open the first part of the waterway from Essington and Bloxwich to Horseley Fields. The Birmingham Canal Navigations were concerned that they would lose water at the junction to the Wyrley Canal. An inspection carried out by their engineers found that the stop lock comprised only two gates and the level on the Wyrley Canal was 8 inches below the level of the Birmingham Canal. The BCN were keen to have a stop lock with four gates so that no water could be lost from their waterway. There was also a clause in the Wyrley Canal Act that required the Wyrley Canal level to be 6 inches higher than that in the Birmingham Canal.

Presently, stop planks had been fastened on the Birmingham Canal side to prevent any traffic passing through, but from November 1794 the communication with the Wyrley & Essington Canal was formally opened. With the navigation open to trade, the BCN pressed the Wyrley Company to build the junction toll-cottage. Traffic was essentially coal boats coming from the collieries.

John Brawn was proceeding with the cutting towards Catshill. He proposed to complete all the work of the bridges (excepting the first bridge at Walsall), all weirs, and drawbridges and stop gates by March 1795, so water could be let in and navigation commenced.

The work again was delayed and by April 1795, Mr Caddick at Brownhills had complained to the committee that the drawbridge on his land was not complete. Brawn was instructed to complete Caddick's drawbridge, and finish several other bridges. During June 1795 the committee went to Lichfield to view to the intended work from there to Huddlesford. Mr Brawn proposed to build the three locks and bridges next to Huddlesford in three months.

John Brawn therefore completed most of the main canal from Wolverhampton to Huddlesford. Construction work on this section was completed during 1797. The canal was opened to traffic throughout on 8 May 1797. William Pitt ceased to be surveyor for the canal company in Christmas 1796, but was paid an additional 50 guineas to complete the survey book, including all settlements with the occupiers of land.

The construction of the final length from Ogley to Huddlesford was different to the Parliamentary plan prepared in 1793. The most notable deviation was the section that passed beside the Tamworth Turnpike Road. The plan had the canal crossing nearer Lichfield and running down the opposite side of the road to which it was finally built.

In July 1798, the committee decided to make a 6-inch stop lock at Sneyd. John Brawn was instructed to make an estimate for building this lock and ordered to proceed with the job.

It was customary for calls to be made at intervals, and thus contractor's fees and land-purchase was financed as needed. Not all share calls were paid, however, and despite frequent requests over £3,000 remained unpaid. This deficit unfortunately delayed completion of the canal. It was a state of affairs which was not tolerated by those who had paid all the calls up front. A letter published in *Aris's Gazette* on 23 June 1800, written by five shareholders, publicly drew attention to the fact that a great neglect had occurred. A special meeting was called at the Swan, Wolverhampton, on 7 July 1800, to find a solution to the problem.

The debts were actually in excess of this amount, and fresh capital to the value of £8,300 was borrowed on mortgage during 1803. But the canal was complete and the potential for local trade on the waterway route as well as through long-distance trade was a revenue-earner.

# Features of Wyrley & Essington Canal
## Birchills–Brownhills–Huddlesford

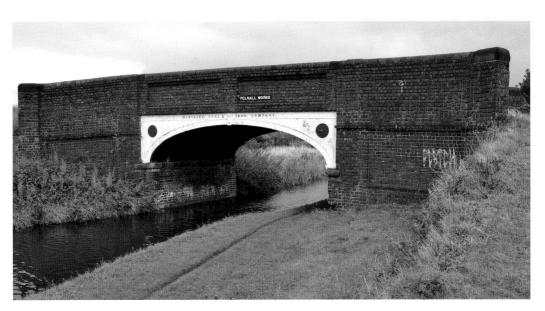

**Pelsall Works Bridge & Detail of Horseley Iron Company Ironworks, 2011**

A survivor from the industrial age is the brick-and-iron Pelsall Works bridge, whose iron structure was provided by the Horseley Iron Company at Tipton. The date carried, of 1824, corresponds with the development of the coal works at Pelsall Wood in that year. The land belonged to the Church of England and the developers of the mineral estate were the Fryer family. Ironworks were established there during 1832. The metal structure of this bridge ranks among the earliest surviving of the Horseley Company of Tipton. The photograph on the left shows the details of the ironwork.

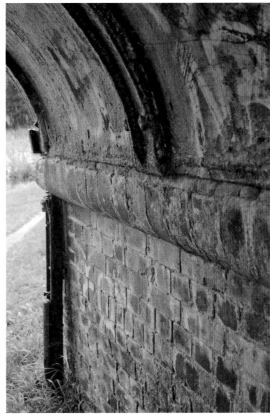

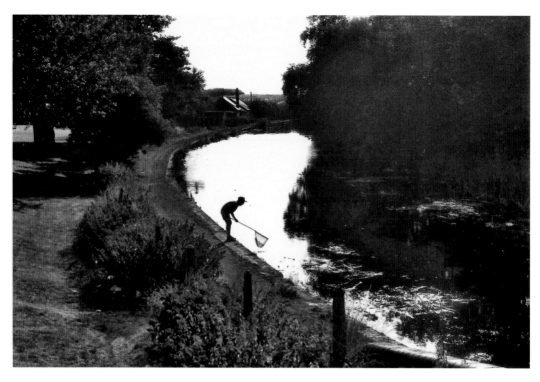

**Wyrley & Essington Canal at Anchor Bridge & Ogley Junction, Brownhills**
(*Above*) The canal followed a curved route around Brownhills to Ogley. (*Below*) When the Wyrley Extension Canal was constructed, the route was from left to right, with a feeder from Cannock Chase Reservoir meeting the canal here. The feeder was reconstructed as a navigable canal between 1850 and 1851 in order to serve new collieries that had been established near the reservoir. The main waterway also descended through a flight of thirty locks here and two canal cottages were constructed beside the top lock. (*Below photograph: Walsall Archives*)

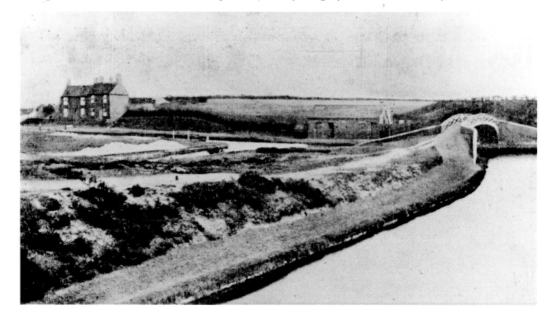

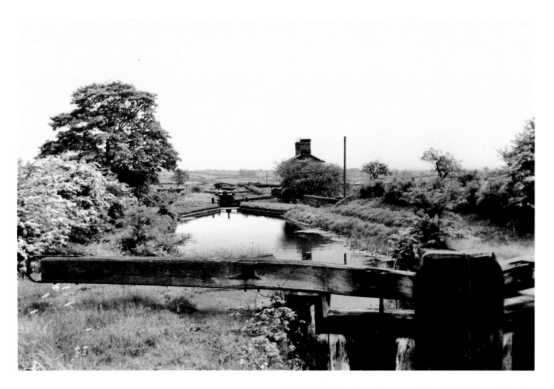

## Lock 4 and Lock House, Ogley Locks & Locks 13–17, Ogley, Near Fosseway

The Ogley Locks were grouped together in a series of lock flights. The first started at Ogley and comprised eight locks.

The Fosseway crossed the canal at the bottom of Lock 17. There were four locks here, arranged along a curved course. Side ponds were provided to assist the conservation of water. The South Staffordshire Railway passed close to these locks. (*Photographs: Arthur Watts*)

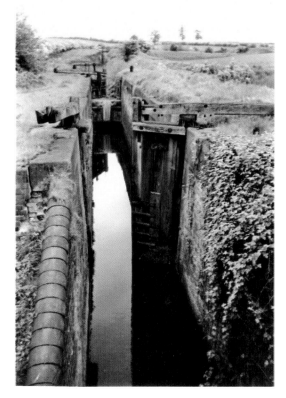

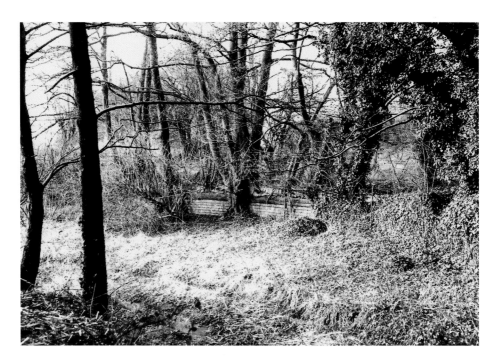

### Pipe Hill Wharf & Pipe Hill Deviation, 1998

The Wyrley & Essington had a number of wharves beside roads for trading boats to call or for the delivery of manure to the farmers. Pipe Hill Wharf was placed beside the main Walsall–Lichfield turnpike.

The making of the South Staffordshire Railway (1847–49) included a diversion of the canal to the south under a new brick bridge that carried the Walsall–Lichfield turnpike over the canal. The Fosseway (*inset*) crossed the South Staffordshire Railway on the level, but went over the canal on the bridge at the tail of Lock 17. While the canal here is presently infilled, the cottage has remained.

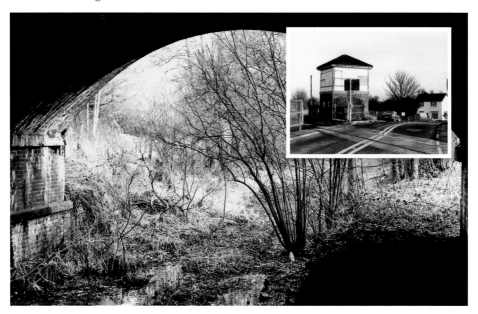

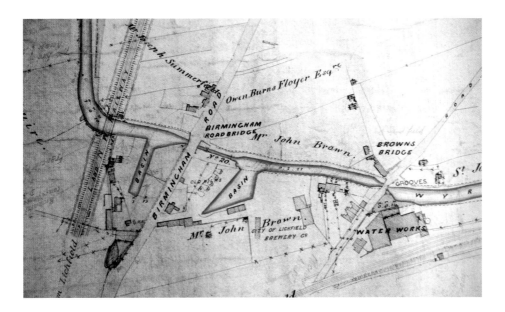

## Plans of Birmingham Road Wharves, Lichfield

Cotterill's survey, the canal from the Waterworks to the Birmingham Road is shown. The original Waterworks building is shown in black, while the red parts represent the future extensions where the later George & Jonah Davies Pumping Engine was installed. The City of Lichfield Brewery malting are also marked in red to show they were erected after 1868. A bank of limekilns has also been added to the wharf principally owned by limemasters, the Brawn family. Joseph Summerfield was the owner and propietor of the Duke of Wellington. Also etched in red is the London & North Western Railway, which formed the extension from Sutton Coldfield that was constructed between 1882 and 1884. (*Below map: Lichfield & Hatherton Canal Trust*)

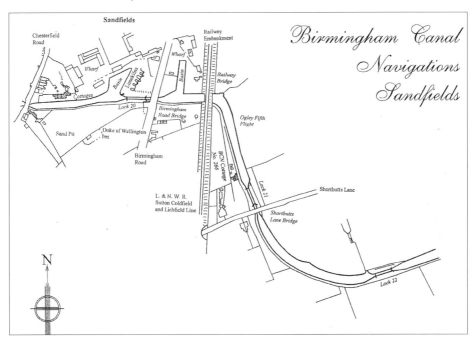

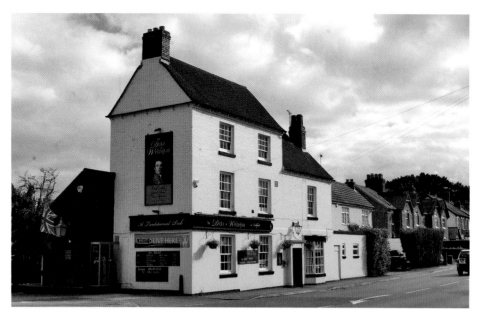

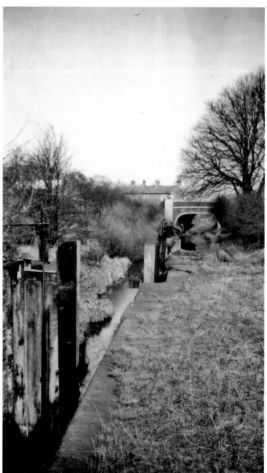

## Duke of Wellington, Birmingham Road & Lock 23, London Road, Lichfield, 1956

(*Above*) The Duke of Wellington was a canal-side public house, which originally had outbuildings. The original structure predates the waterway that passed close by. It also faced the former turnpike that crossed the canal by a bridge here. These buildings were once used as a slaughterhouse. They became a public house early in the nineteenth century and there was a case where a body was dragged from the canal and the deceased was left in the upper storey of the outbuildings prior to the inquest at this house. In modern times there have been reports of a ghost being seen descending through the bar, as if coming from the upper floor of the now-demolished outbuildings into the cellar below. (*Left*) The canal descended after Lock 23 to pass under the London Road. There was a basin to the left that was known as St John's Wharf. Beyond the bridge on the left was London Road Wharf. (*Railway & Canal Historical Society Ref 65996*)

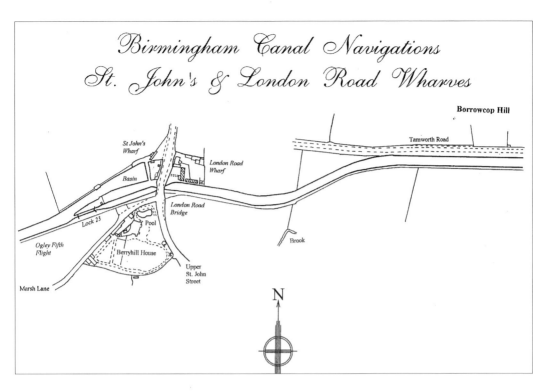

*Birmingham Canal Navigations*
*St. John's & London Road Wharves*

**Ogley Lock 23 & Huddlesford, 1998**
A section of the Wyrley & Essington Canal between the junction with the Coventry Canal and Cappers Lane was adopted as long-term moorings for the Lichfield Cruising Club. (*Above map: Lichfield & Hatherton Canal Trust*)

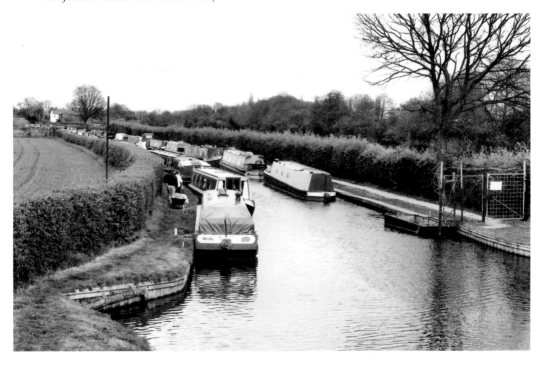

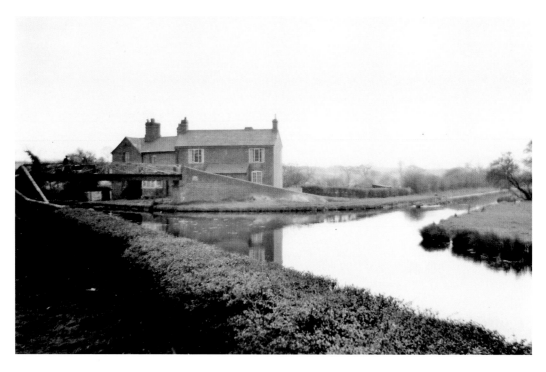

### Huddlesford Junction, 1955 & 1998
The Wyrley & Essington joined the Coventry Canal at Huddlesford, where a turnover bridge was provided to carry the towpath over the Coventry Canal to enable boat-horses to cross over. (*Above photograph: Railway & Canal Historical Society Ref 65998*)

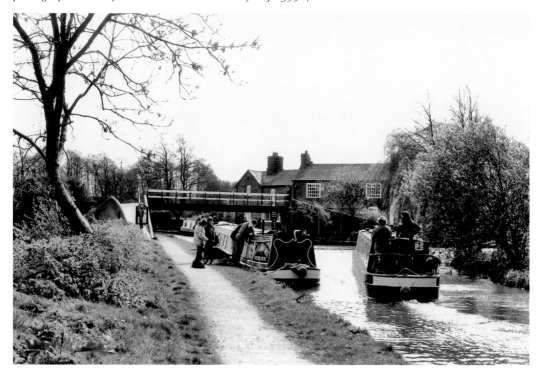

# Wyrley & Essington
## Canal Branches

Work was then concentrated on the two main branches to Hay Head and Lords Hayes. That to Hay Head was constructed as surveyed. The other line was altered to terminate at Newtown and never reached the quarries belonging to Lords Hayes.

Henry Vernon was evidently not satisfied with the transport arrangements made for his coal and in 1798 commissioned Thomas Dadford to survey a railroad from his New Colliery, Essington, to the Staffordshire & Worcestershire Canal near Calf Heath. Vernon's application to Parliament to make the railway was opposed by the Wyrley & Essington Canal Company. The railway was not built, but considerable ill feeling persisted between Vernon and the canal company for a number of years.

Partial appeasement came in the form a railway which was to link the New Colliery with the proposed Lords Hayes Branch. In June 1799 Mr Bishton (William?), surveyor, was requested to cost the railway and the same to be laid down under the direction of Mr Bishton and Mr Clare.

In May 1799, John Brawn was instructed to finish up all his work and put the canal in a perfect state of repair. His son, John Brawn, junior, who had no doubt helped him on his various projects, was also appointed engineer and surveyor to the Wyrley & Essington Canal Company.

The reservoir at Sneyd burst its banks in June 1799. The effects of this accident were to delay work elsewhere as repairs to the reservoir and canal were carried out. In September Mr Brawn (senior?) was authorised to cut and puddle the Lords Hayes Branch, while John Brawn, junior, was required to employ a sufficient number of men to throw up the ground for Mr Vernon's railway on, or before, 5 October.

Work on the Daw End Branch Canal to Hay Head is rarely mentioned in the surviving minutes, but by November 1800 the committee were urging its completion. How much of this work was done by John Brawn, senior, is not certain, because by now the rigours of canal construction had begun to take their toll on him. John Brawn, senior, died in May 1801. John Brawn, junior, carried out any outstanding work on the main line and the branches. The canal was finally announced as being complete on 30 November 1801.

The Daw End, or Hay Head, Branch, which joined the main Wyrley & Essington Canal at Catshill, was made to serve the lime works at Rushall and Hay Head. The route was somewhat circuitous as it passed through Walsall Wood and near to Aldridge before turning westward for Rushall. It seems that part remained unfinished by November 1800, and it is not certain when the outstanding work was done, although it was most likely finished in 1801. The Daw End Canal remained a branch waterway until 1846, when the majority of its course was incorporated into a new through route from the Tame Valley Canal to the collieries on Cannock Chase.

John Brawn, junior, was retained as engineer through to 1802, when the company advertised for a new engineer. Richard Stevens was appointed and retained this post through to 1840, when the Wyrley & Essington Canal was merged with the Birmingham Canal Navigations.

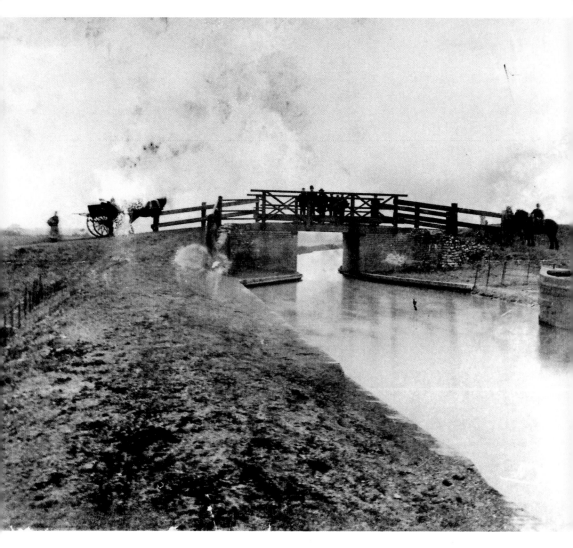

**Fishley No. 1 Bridge, Lords Hayes Branch**
Much of the land around the Lords Hayes Branch was level and bridge approaches were banked up for carts and wagons to pass over the canal. At this bridge the towing path changed sides and the bridge hole was only wide enough to pass a narrow boat. The bridge in this view was made of timber and the reason for the people standing on the bridge and bridge approaches appears to be a fire. (*Photograph: Walsall Archives*)

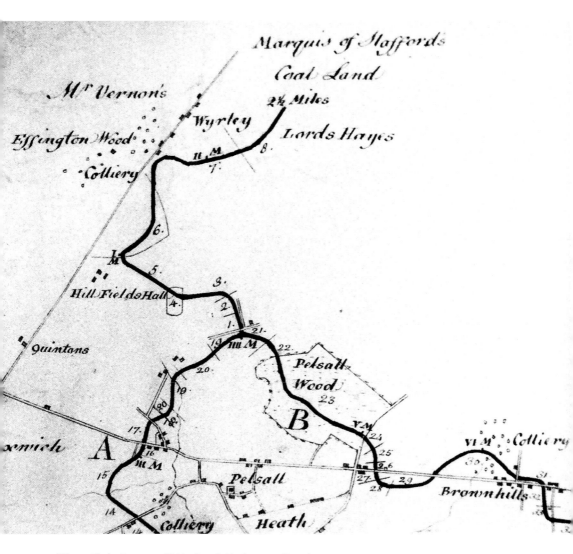

**William Pitt's Survey of Wyrley & Essington Canal, 1793**

The intended route of the branch to Lords Hayes was to reach the mines belonging to the Marquis of Stafford. The route was, however, changed to turn west to the mines on Essington Wood Colliery, where a tramway was built by the Wyrley & Essington Canal Company to mines on the west side of the estate.

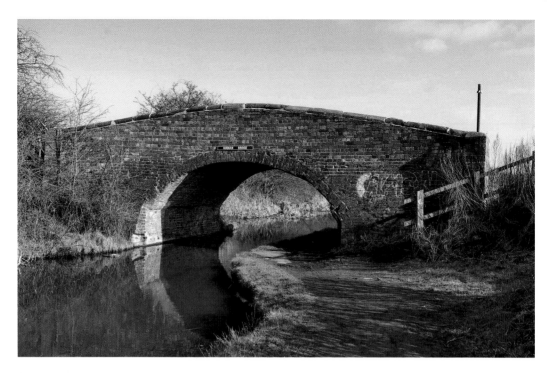

**Riddian's Bridge & Winterley Bridge, 2011**
Riddian's Bridge is a typical Wyrley & Essington bridge which was probably built at the time of the making of the Daw End Canal. Winterley Bridge is a more substantial structure that may have been altered.

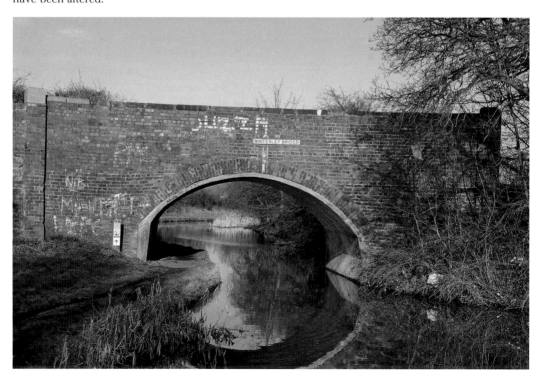

# Water Supplies
## The Early Years, 1792–1823

The provision of water was essential to the working of any canal and adequate supplies had to be gained to facilitate to movement of traffic. The problem for any engineer planning a new waterway was to secure that supply. William Pitt provided the survey and also suggested the method of water supply. His plans, first formulated in 1791 and revised in 1792 and 1793, were published as a printed map in 1793. They show two reservoirs: one at Essington Wood (Sneyd) and another near Catshill.

There were also culverts where water was diverted from streams or mine engines. The supply from streams was limited, as the landowners frequently jealously guarded these rights for the mill owners.

The Sneyd Reservoir supplied water into the upper-summit level (503 feet OD) between Sneyd and Old Essington Wood Colliery. While this section was under construction, the committee sanctioned the purchase of a Whimsey Engine. This steam engine was to be used to pump water up to the upper-summit level and no doubt enabled the upper level to be filled with enough water to move the construction traffic. Henry Vernon could pump water into the canal from his mine, or pumping engines, located at Old and New Essington Colliery. In this latter case, payment would be made for the water.

Sneyd Reservoir was not completed in time for the opening of the line to Wolverhampton. On 1 December 1794, it was reported that Mr Hanson was sure to finish the reservoir in one month. The reservoir at Sneyd, which drew water from the neighbouring land, would have been completed therefore by January 1795.

Water levels in the lower level were, at first, not as high as expected. The Birmingham Canal Navigations Company were particularly keen that they should be 6 inches higher than their own (473 feet OD). There are several mentions made in the BCN committee meetings that this was not the case and water was being lost from the Birmingham Canal summit level. When levels in the Wyrley Canal were particularly low, the Birmingham Canal Company simply closed the communication. The BCN were insistent that a second pair of stop lock gates were constructed at Horseley Fields Junction. Those presently installed only worked to the favour of the Wyrley Company.

Matters finally came to a head in April 1796. The Birmingham Canal Navigation Company had clearly shown restraint in its dealings with the Wyrley & Essington Canal Company, but finding that after some eighteen months of operation no action had been taken over the stop lock issue, new instructions were issued to their agent, Mr Brookes, at Horseley Fields Junction. He was ordered to secure the navigation and prevent the passage of boats when the water in the Wyrley & Essington Canal was not up to the height required by the Act of Parliament. Any person attempting to force open the communication when not up to the required level would be prosecuted. Eight boats did force a passage through on 9 April when the height of water was not up to the level required by law. Prosecutions were made out for people guilty of the offence.

These closures must have had an effect on trade and the mood of the canal traders caught up in the dispute between the two canal companies. Boatmen received payment for the journey made, and enforced stoppages such as those imposed by the Birmingham Canal Navigations would have cost them money. Their protestations as well as boat owners forced the Wyrley

& Essington Committee to act. They sent their secretary, Thomas D. Wightwick, and William Taylor, to attend the next BCN committee meeting to request some respite, where it was suggested that the BCN agent should forgo closing the navigation when water levels fell below the Parliamentary level (that is 6 inches above the BCN) and only close the waterway when levels fell below those of the Birmingham Canal. This was agreed and instructions issued to Mr Brookes accordingly.

Other diplomatic efforts set in motion a new dialogue concerning the Horsley Field Stop issue. Meanwhile, the Wyrley & Essington Company looked at means of improving their water supply. In April 1796 they ordered that the remaining old shafts in Essington Wood Reservoir, that is Sneyd, should be puddled first. This reference is the first suggestion that the reservoir had occupied old colliery ground and might account for the low water levels experienced. Another reason was the leakages from the new canal, which John Brawn was instructed to rectify.

Mr Hunt, from the BCN, attended the next half-yearly meeting of the Wyrley & Essington proprietors, where an order was issued for the construction of a stop lock at Horseley Field similar to that at Dudley. In May 1796, John Brawn was told to prepare for putting up the stop gates at Wolverhampton Junction. One month later, in June, arrangements were made with the construction of the new stop lock. Mr Bull, from the BCN, attended the works, which were done in a satisfactory manner. Despite Mr Bull's assurances, water still escaped from the BCN into the Wyrley Canal at times, the gates still needed attention from time to time and the navigation continued to be closed on the occasions where loss of water from the BCN was suspected.

Three years later another water problem, of a different nature, was to befall the proprietors of the Wyrley Canal. Sneyd Reservoir may not have been made in a satisfactory manner. The strong rains experienced during May and early June 1799 led to Sneyd Reservoir bursting its banks.

The task of repairing the damage fell to the Brawn family. John Brawn, junior, was given the task of putting the feeder for carrying water into Essington Wood Reservoir and the Reservoir Cross Dams into repair.

Work had already started on a second reservoir to supply the lower level and Ogley locks. Pitt's original suggestion of a reservoir near Catshill appears to have been discounted in favour of one at Norton Bog. An early reference to the Great Reservoirs at Cannock Wood appears in May 1797, when the committee requested Brawn build two small bridges for sheep over the feeders for the Great Reservoirs. Another mention was given in August 1798, when the lower plug for the Great Reservoir at Cannock Wood was drawn on Monday 10 September. The rains that damaged the Sneyd Reservoir dam had perhaps a more serious effect on the dam under construction at Cannock Wood: 'On Wednesday last, the embankment of the reservoir of the Wyrley & Essington Canal on Cannock Heath gave way, and the water swept everything before it in the line it took through Shenstone, Hopwas, Drayton, &c, till it fell into the Tame at Tamworth. At Blackbrook, seven miles from the reservoir, the new stone bridge was blown up; numbers of sheep and some cattle were drowned:- but two or three persons, aware of the accident, at first, rode forward, and giving the farmers alarm, they had time to remove the chief of their cattle and horses to high ground. The damage sustained is, however, very great, and calculated at many thousands of pounds. At Hammerwich, near Lichfield, the meadows are twelve inches deep with the gravel the water brought down with it.'

Unlike Sneyd, the reservoir and feeder was still to be completed. Repair began, but there was now increased urgency to supply water to the main line and the branch under construction to Hay Head. John Brawn, junior, was told to get as many men as he could to complete the Cannock Chase Reservoir.

The task of engineering the dam and reservoir at Cannock Wood was given to Thomas Dadford. By November 1800 it was reported that the banks of the reservoir, 'under Mr Dadford', were to be fenced in stone.

Cannock Wood Reservoir would have been completed by 1801 and a plan for this period shows the dam to enclose an area of 81 acres, 1 rood and 3 perches. The feeder to the main canal passed under the Brownhills to Burton Road to a small reservoir of 8 acres, 1 rood and 2 perches in area. The feeder then went through a short tunnel and then an open cut to cross under Watling Street before flowing into the canal above Ogley Locks.

The following year, in 1802, consideration was given to raising the dam at Cannock Wood and contractors were sought. This work appears to have been carried out, but thereafter little was done to alter the size of the reservoir. In 1818, repairs were authorised.

By 1823, the area of Cannock Wood Reservoir amounted to 150 acres and the Wyrley & Essington Canal Company had sufficient water for their needs and could even sell water to other canal companies. Trade on the Birmingham Canal Navigations by 1823 was increasing, and by this date they were keen to obtain more water. They approached the Wyrley & Essington Company to effect an agreement for their surplus supply.

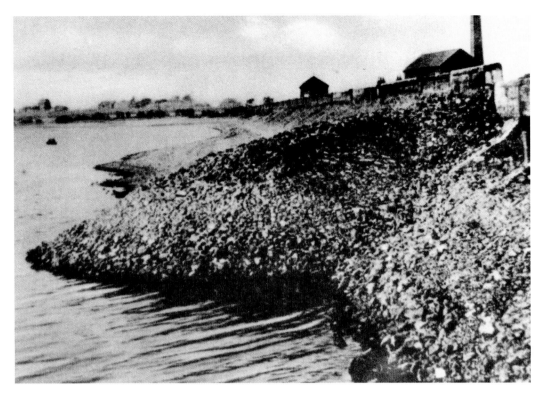

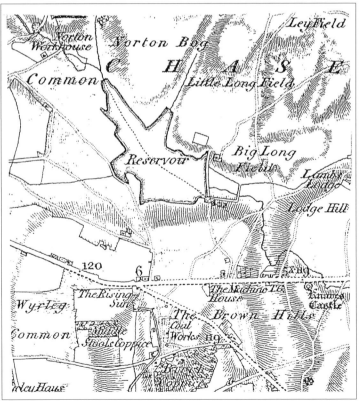

## Cannock Chase Reservoir

This reservoir was slowly fed by streams and springs. The BCN installed a pumping engine, in 1855, to return water to the reservoir when water levels were high. (*Left*) a plan of Cannock Chase Reservoir, 1834. Cannock Chase Reservoir drew water from streams that drained into the reservoir. The feeder to the canal followed a winding course to meet the canal near the top lock, Ogley. (*Reproduced from Ordnance Survey*)

# Chapter Two

# Trade & Operation

Mining was already established at Brownhills, where coal mines and ironstone mines had been drained by a Newcomen Engine and whose produce had been sent by road.

Trade developed at Bloxwich, Birchills, Essington, Rushall and Wednesfield. The principal traffic was coal, but there were also bricks, ironstone and limestone supplementing the traffic. Some merchandise-carriers travelling between Wolverhampton and the East Midlands also used the canal serving Derby and Shardlow, with onward transfer to Gainsborough and the vessels that sailed along the East Coast to London, the North East or Scotland.

## Coal Trade

Coal mining was carried on at Essington, Birchills and Brownhills, where the measures nearest the surface were worked.

## Iron Making

Prior to the canal being made there was a charcoal blast furnace at Rushall that smelted local ores, such as were found at the Delves. With the development of the coke-smelting process, ores were carried by road to the first South Staffordshire furnaces. The making of the Wyrley & Essington assisted this trade. There were supplies of ironstone mined in the Birchills area and this led to the establishment of a furnace at Birchills (Old Birchills). Ironstone mining was also conducted near Heath Town and New Cross, Wednesfield.

## Limestone Trade

Limestone was quarried and mined near Rushall, at Moss Close, Daw End and Linley. Hay Head at the end of the branch also produced a limestone that was suitable for making cement. The limestone was principally used for building purposes or a flux in the iron-smelting purposes.

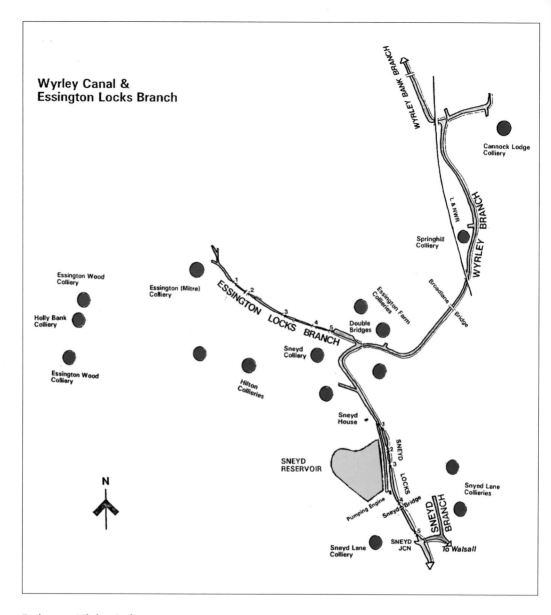

## Essington Mining Industry

The initial focus of the Wyrley & Essington Canal was the mines at Essington. To reach these mines the canal climbed through five locks to the Wyrley Level, to which Sneyd Reservoir supplied water. Mines were located in the Essington Wood area, bringing coal from the seams nearest the surface. The Essington Branch Canal brought boats up to a higher level, and one that drew on local watercourses for a supply. In later times, other mines were developed.

# Alternative Schemes
## & Private Branches

The Wyrley & Essington competed for Walsall traffic with the Birmingham Canal Navigations. They were the first canal to serve Walsall, but passed to the north of the town. The Birmingham & Fazeley Canal obtained powers to extend their canal from Broadwaters to Park Street, Walsall, in 1794. This same Act also gave permission for the company to simplify its name to the Birmingham Canal Navigations. They had planned another branch from Broadwaters through Bilston to Wolverhampton, joining their summit level near Walsall Street Bridge. This proposal was not adopted, but the canal through to Walsall was completed in 1799. The nearest the Wyrley & Essington Canal came to the centre of Walsall was Birchills Wharf, which was located at the end of the Birchills Branch.

Traffic on the Wyrley & Essington Canal never reached its true potential while it remained in independent ownership and, in fact, showed signs of decline during the 1820s and 1830s. Those who possessed mineral properties were keen to establish links between the Birmingham Canal Navigations and the Wyrley & Essington Canal to improve trade. Yet the only connections with any other waterway were made at Horseley Fields and Huddlesford. It seems that the Birmingham Canal Navigations resisted any prospect of further union, which proved detrimental to trade developing further.

One such scheme was the Birmingham, Walsall & Liverpool Junction Canal, which was first proposed on 1 November 1825 and comprised three separate lengths of waterway. This was an ambitious project that commenced near the centre of Birmingham at Walmer Lane (later Lancaster Street), where a junction was made with the Birmingham & Fazeley Canal. It was then to pass through Perry Barr, Great Barr, Bescot, Caldmore, Walsall and Birchills where it joined the Wyrley & Essington Canal. The second section left the Wyrley & Essington near Pelsall and travelled northwards through Wyrley and then turned down through Churchbridge, Saredon and Gailey to join the Staffordshire & Worcestershire Canal at Otherton. The third part diverged from the Staffordshire & Worcestershire Canal at Baswich and joined the Trent & Mersey Canal at Stone.

Richard Fryer was a promoter for this venture and, like James Hordern, was a Wolverhampton banker. Fryer had also taken an interest in land at Pelsall, where he was about to establish collieries, and the new scheme promised better transport for his goods. A meeting of landowners and others interested in the scheme was held at the George Hotel, Walsall, on 22 September 1826. Edward Littleton MP presided. It was stated that 200,000 acres of coal, ironstone and limestone, now unproductive, would be brought into operation and consumption. The proposed canal would shorten conveyance through the saving of many locks.

Representatives from the Birmingham, Staffordshire & Worcestershire and Wyrley & Essington Canals all attended and it was mentioned that their surveyors were contemplating a junction of the lines of their canals. In the course of things this junction proved to be a long way off, but this statement was enough to cause an adjournment of the meeting, to give time for these surveys to be prepared.

It is now a matter of historical record that some of these canals were made. The Tame Valley (1844) and Rushall (1846) Canals followed a roughly similar route to that proposed, linking Birmingham with the undeveloped coalfields alluded to in 1826. The Staffordshire &

Worcestershire Canal Company completed the Hatherton Branch to Churchbridge in 1841, while the Wyrley Bank Canal reached other parts of the Wyrley Coalfield. Later, in 1863, the Churchbridge Locks were opened and forged a new link between the Hartherton Branch and the Cannock Extension Canal. The only part not built was the link between the Staffordshire & Worcestershire Canal and the Trent & Mersey. The purpose for this canal became less relevant with the completion of the Birmingham & Liverpool Junction Canal.

The proposals were discussed at the Wyrley & Essington Canal proprietors' meeting in May 1827. There was an enthusiastic response concerning the links proposed between the Wyrley & Essington Canal and the Birmingham Canal Navigations. The link from Pelsall to the Staffordshire & Worcestershire Canal met with a less favourable response. In their opinion, 'it was not at the present time advisable for company to make such communication'.

Enthusiasm for the Birmingham, Walsall & Liverpool Junction Canal waned as other projects, notably public railways, captured the investor's capital. The Birmingham Canal Navigations entered into fresh negotiations with the Wyrley & Essington Canal Company to secure a merger between the two concerns and finally, in 1839, agreed terms for consolidation. As a separate issue, plans had already been made for linking the Birmingham Canal with the Wyrley through Bentley in order to serve the rich coal and ironstone fields located there. Plans were also now proposed for a second link, joining the Daw End Canal with the Tame Valley. In fact, adjustments were made to the route of the Tame Valley Canal to affect a better link.

The shortest connection between the two waterways was actually at Walsall, but the Birmingham Canal committee for some reason resisted this junction. Proposals to build a junction at Walsall had been suggested in 1825, when John Clements Whateley and other owners and occupiers of mines suggested the canal link. The response of the canal committee was that a survey had been ordered and that they were not prepared to enter into a discussion on the subject until it was completed.

The industrialists and townspeople of Walsall made a more vociferous attempt in 1829. Another request was made in 1834, all to no avail. In 1837 the junction was proposed for the third time, apparently with the backing of the Birmingham Canal Navigations. The slow progress encountered with these final negotiations eventually stimulated an independent group to make the canal. A connection between the Birchills Branch and the Walsall Canal was formally proposed in December 1838, when a share issue was offered for the Walsall Junction Canal. A group of businessmen, including local coal-masters William Hanbury, junior & James Smallman and lime master John Bradnock Adams, had got together to promote the link as a private venture. James Frost, who was already engaged on building the Stourbridge Extension Canal, engineered the plan for the intended canal link.

In addition to the main canal there were four private branch canals, which connected with the main canal:

## Pelsall Works
This branch canal was built around 1826 to serve Pelsall Common collieries, belonging to Richard Fryer. It ceased to have any function after the Pelsall Ironworks were enlarged by the Bloomer family.

## Gilpin's Arm
Built in 1811 to serve a part of Pelsall Coal Works that belonged to William James & Co. Other subsequent users included the Gilpin family and the Pelsall Coal & Iron Company.

## Sandhill's Arm
Built to serve the estate and farm that belonged to George and James Brawn.

## Slough Arm
Built probably as early as 1797 to serve the coal works that belonged to Phineas Hussey at Brownhills.

## Sneyd Branch
A short branch east of Sneyd Junction that served ironstone and coal mines.

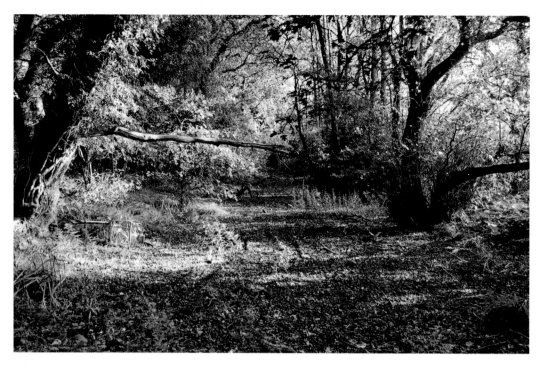

### Slough Arm & Engine Lane Bridge

Dry bed of the arm looking towards the lock from Engine Lane Bridge. While the private Slough Arm has been disused for many years, it still acts a watercourse, where a stream flows down to join up with the northern tributaries of the River Tame. Such waters were of help in maintaining the navigation to the colliery wharves.

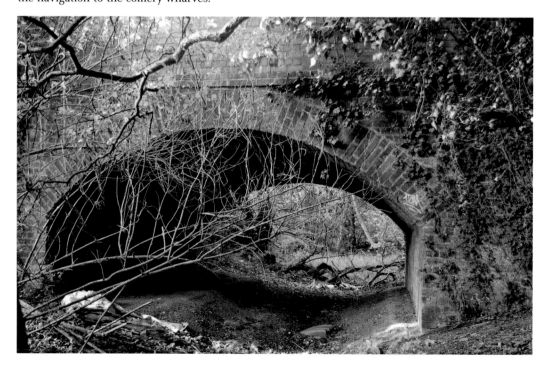

# Chapter Three

# Mergers & Expansion

There is evidence to suggest that trade on the Wyrley & Essington Canal never reached its full potential. The collieries at Essington had closed and elsewhere coal mining was carried on at a limited scale. The state of the waterway also appears to have deteriorated, with shoals accumulating in certain places and restricting navigation. They did have one important resource: water. The two reservoirs at Sneyd and Cannock Wood were more than capable of supplying the water for trade then carried on the canal, and there was water to spare.

Messrs Wightwick, Buckle, Warner and Clare were appointed to assist the committee in November 1822 in investigating the decline in tonnage carried along the line of the canal. Part of their brief was to look at all new avenues and channels of trade available, what best use could be made of any surplus water and any prudent and practical suggestions.

A union between the Wyrley & Essington Canal and the Birmingham Canal were proposed as early as 1820. Committees had met but could not find suitable grounds for merger.

Renewed attempts were made for merger, in 1830. The previous year, the Wyrley & Essington Company received a petition from local landowners, mine owners, coal-masters, ironmasters, carriers and residents of the town of Walsall, who all wanted a junction made between the Wyrley & Essington and the Birmingham Canal at Walsall. Such a large deputation must have been of deep concern to the canal committee. A special committee was appointed but, after six months, their deliberations had not yet 'matured'.

The Wyrley & Essington Canal Company was in a difficult position, as any new project, as far as they were concerned, required Parliamentary approval. It was decided at the earliest opportunity to open a Treaty for Union of the Wyrley & Essington with the Birmingham Canal Navigations.

This time the Birmingham Canal committee welcomed the merger and committees were set up to work towards it. Yet it seems these negotiations failed again. Meanwhile, other applications for a junction canal at Walsall were tendered. Richard Fryer, proprietor of the Pelsall Ironworks, was one who asked for the junction canal to be cut in 1834.

Merger talks appear to have been hampered through various factors; the value of shares, perhaps, being the most important consideration. The routes of the new junction canals were also undecided. Some people, including the BCN surveyor, doubted the value of making some of them. There also appeared to be two political factions among the Wyrley & Essington proprietors: those who favoured union and those who did not.

The biggest asset Wyrley & Essington had was the water supply, and this card was played at every negotiation meeting to get the best for the Wyrley & Essington shareholders. The records of the proprietors' meetings are sometimes brief and much is left out. More can be obtained of this interchange from the Birmingham Canal Navigations records.

There was a continuing dispute over water. The Wyrley & Essington Canal Acts had allocated any spare water to the Birmingham Canal. But the Wyrley & Essington Company wanted to sell as much as possible for revenue. The issue of 'spare' water was a frequent cause of complaint and legal proceedings were threatened at one point by the committee of the Birmingham Canal Navigations.

Another deputation from Walsall, which included Mr Finch MP, had approached the Birmingham Canal committee in September 1837 to renew attempts to make a junction between the two canals at Walsall. This deputation then attended the next Wyrley & Essington proprietors' meeting to deliver the Birmingham Canal Navigations' response. The message was conveyed that the Birmingham Canal Navigations were now willing to make a canal at their own expense out of the canal at Walsall, or from the end of the Anson's Branch, to Birchills. George Benjamin Thorneycroft also reported that the Birmingham Canal Navigations wanted to make another canal from the lower level near Darlaston to the Wyrley & Essington Canal at Wednesfield. There were thus serious intentions by the Birmingham Canal Company to strengthen the links with the Wyrley & Essington Canal.

Among the Wyrley & Essington proprietors were a group that favoured the junction proposals, while there were others who appeared to be against any form of additional union with the Birmingham Canal. Those who were keen to make the new junction line at Walsall met together at the house of Mr Cotterill, in Lichfield Street, Walsall. Here they formulated three resolutions that were to form the basis for the working of the junction canals when built. These rules were formulated on the basis of the Birmingham Canal Navigations building the canals and collecting the tolls. The water was to be provided by the Wyrley & Essington Company generally free of charge. These resolutions, which were reproduced in the proprietors' minutes, were to provide the stimulus of greater events. After these suggestions were presented to the Birmingham Canal Company, the complete merger between the Birmingham and Wyrley Canals was yet again suggested.

A report concerning this proposed merger, compiled by John Freeth (secretary), J. Brogden and C. Ingleby during July 1838, led to negotiations with the Wyrley Company being resumed. A select committee was asked to investigate the matter. The main point of issue was the value of the Wyrley & Essington Canal shares, which were worth less than those for the Birmingham Canal Navigations. Discussions were terminated because both parties failed to agree.

At the statutory meeting of Wyrley & Essington proprietors, held in November 1838, it was decided that negotiations should be continued. Committees were reformed for both parties. The Birmingham Canal committee, which comprised Messrs Browne, Merry, Hunt, Galton and Scott, had discussions with the Wyrley committee, composed of Messrs Stokes, Thorneycroft, Briscoe, Hordern, Ward, Wightwick and Rutter. The Birmingham team suggested that each share of the Wyrley & Essington Canal should be subject to a payment of £70. The Wyrley committee declined this offer. The Birmingham committee then suggested £60 a share, but the Wyrley people offered £44 for consolidation. The Birmingham people declined this, and matters remained deadlocked. Meanwhile, a canal Bill was prepared by a group of Walsall businessmen to make the Walsall Junction Canal independently.

George Benjamin Thorneycroft personally approached John Freeth to renew negotiations. Thorneycroft was an ironmaster who had works at Wolverhampton and his intervention led to fresh discussions with the Wyrley & Essington chairman, John Stokes. An agreement was finally made on 9 February 1839 when Robert Scott, for the BCN, and John Stokes, for the Wyrley & Essington, set the value of Wyrley & Essington shares at £49. Formal permission for the merger was then left for the respective proprietors meetings to agree.

The Wyrley & Essington proprietors' meeting, which took place on 2 March 1839, approved the merger. The Birmingham Canal proprietors met on 5 March at the Navigation Offices in Birmingham and also agreed. Prior to the vote, the reasons for the merger with the Wyrley Canal were laid out. Two advantages were specifically mentioned: the considerable difficulty of supplying water for the increased trade would be alleviated and the pressing need for supplying the Willenhall district could also be resolved.

A number of ironworks in the Wolverhampton and Bilston districts were working minerals, particularly the ironstone measures, on the intervening lands between their works and Willenhall. Railways were laid down and constantly extended. It was felt that a canal link through this area would benefit the Birmingham Canal Navigations. The merger negotiations of 1838 corresponded with the renewed interest in serving the Willenhall district.

While the merger was first agreed by the 9 February document, Parliamentary approval also had to be secured. From February 1839, both companies effectively worked as one, but the legal merger was a year away. The draft application was prepared and initially considered together with the proposed Bentley, Tame Valley and Rushall Canals. By November, it had been decided to make the union between the two companies a separate Bill.

The proprietors of the Wyrley & Essington Canal continued to hold their statutory meetings until 1840. The last was held at the Swan Inn, Wolverhampton, on 2 April 1840. The Act for Consolidating the Wyrley & Essington Canal Navigations with the Birmingham Canal Navigations received Royal Assent on 14 April 1840.

From April 1840, the canal, lands and infrastructure, which had formerly belonged to the Wyrley & Essington Canal Company, were absorbed into the greater Birmingham Canal system, becoming No. 4 maintenance district of that concern.

# Water Supplies from 1823

The Wyrley & Essington Company tried to realise as much revenue as possible from the water contained in the two reservoirs at Cannock Chase and Sneyd. The Birmingham Canal Navigations were keen to get any spare water from the Wyrley Canal. This was a period immediately before the services of Thomas Telford were secured, who between 1825 and 1830 made considerable improvements to that canal's supply of water.

Cannock Chase Reservoir then covered 150 acres, but the supply from the springs was limited. The BCN offered £1,000 per year for exclusive rights to this reservoir and also suggested that an increase of dam height would increase supply. These negotiations evidently failed to progress to an actual agreement and water supply to the Birmingham Canal remained a contentious issue. The flow of water over the weir at Wolverhampton into the Birmingham Canal was minimal and despite alterations to this weir water continued to be lost over weirs east of Wednesfield.

Solicitors' letters were exchanged, but little was done to increase the volume passing over the Horseley Fields Weir. By April 1838, the option of taking legal proceedings was considered by the BCN committee. They were, however, reluctant to take this step and decided to let the solicitors argue the case. In September 1838, the Wyrley & Essington Canal sold 1,000 locks of water to the Birmingham & Liverpool Junction Canal at 5 shillings per lock. The BCN solicitors were again instructed to pursue the right of surplus water and to obtain compensation for the water sold. Within a few months the problem of the water dispute became an academic one, with the completion of merger negotiations. Once the two groups of proprietors ratified the merger in March 1839, the reservoirs at Cannock Chase and Sneyd became the property of the joint-concern.

The Birmingham Canal Navigations enlarged both Sneyd and Cannock Reservoirs. Sneyd, at 510 feet above OD, was enlarged in 1849 to give a surface area of 19 acres. In 1854, a steam pump was erected to lift water from the 473-foot level into the reservoir. Mining subsidence affected the dam reservoirs and these had to be raised in 1883. Cannock Chase Reservoir dam was raised at various dates (1854, 1865, 1874 and 1886), which increased the reservoir surface area to 233 acres. Back-pumping from the 473-foot level was made possible in 1855 when a steam-pumping engine, placed in a building adjacent to the reservoir, commenced work.

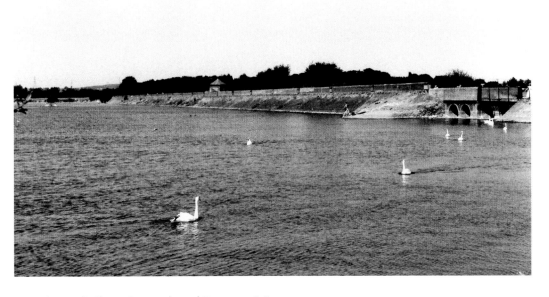

Cannock Chase Reservoir and Dam, 1998 & 2010
(*Above*) Cannock Chase Reservoir suffered from mining subsidence and this led to the dam being built up to maintain levels. Birmingham Canal Navigations later added a dam on the north-west side and increased the area of water storage. (*Below*) The reservoir was drained in 2010 in order to repair the dam walls. The contractor Galliford Try was subsequently appointed to carry out the repairs, which were completed during April 2012.

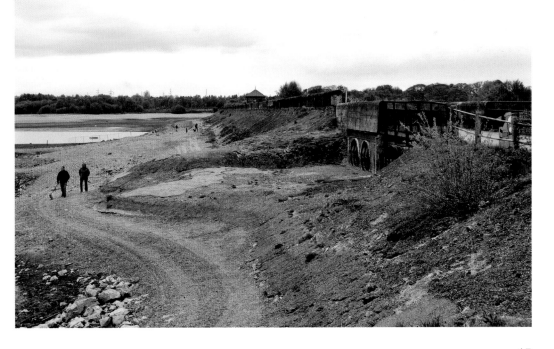

# BCN Improvements

Following the merger of the Birmingham and Wyrley canals, the BCN was faced with the task of upgrading the Wyrley & Essington. It was a task that involved the reconstruction of locks along the Ogley Locks flight.

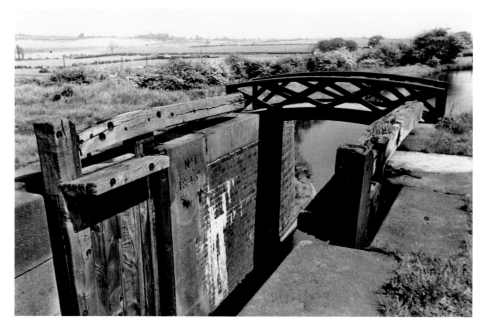

**Ogley Lock 1 & Lock 26 Date Stone, 2012**
Lock 1 bears the date 1845, when the BCN rebuilt this structure. The date stone for Lock 26 was removed, but is presently stored on ground nearby. (*Above photograph: Arthur Watts*)

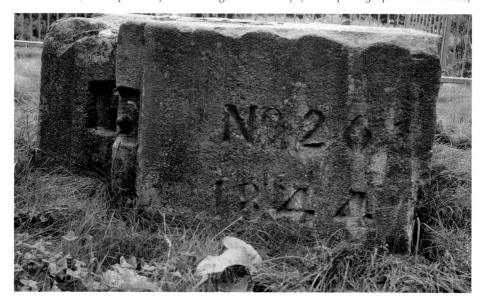

# Southern Connections

Three important links were made between 1841 and 1847 and provided new connections between the Birmingham Canal Navigations and the Wyrley & Essington Canal.

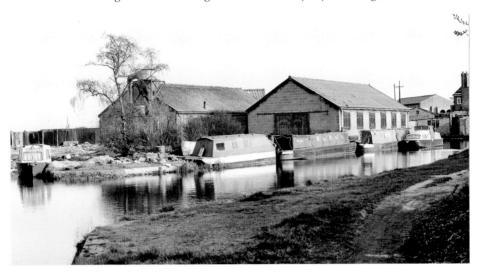

**Walsall Junction Canal and Birchills Branch, 1983 & Toll-House 204, Walsall Top Lock**
The Walsall Junction Canal joined the Wyrley & Essington Canal near the terminus of the Birchills Branch. The Birchills Branch continued on to the end of the branch at Birchills Wharf. The distinctive cottage and toll-house 204 was next to the boatman's mission and the site of the former pumping station, which recirculated water between the bottom of the locks and the top.

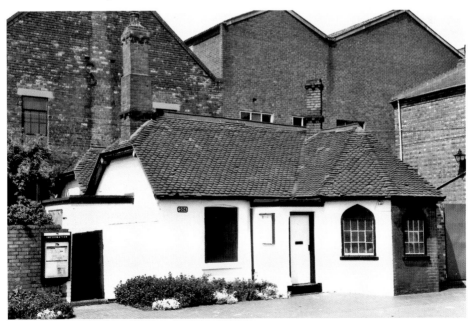

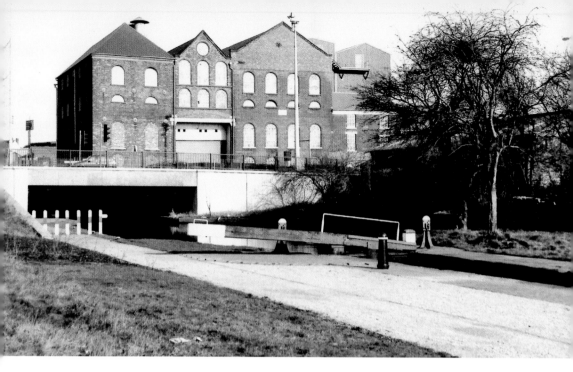

Walsall Bottom Lock and Smiths Flour Mill & Bentley Canal, Junction with Wyrley & Essington at New Cross

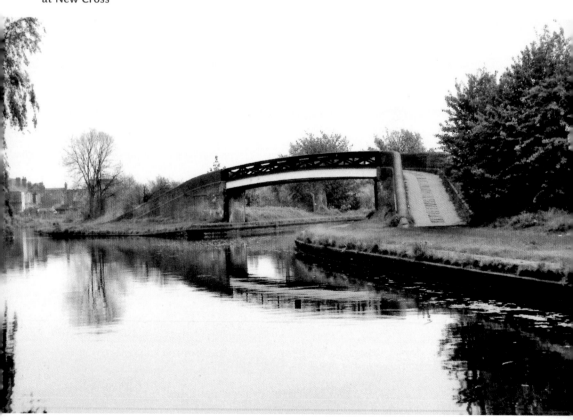

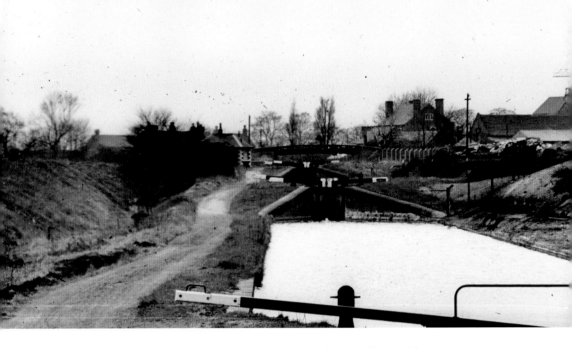

Locks 1–3, Bentley Canal at Wednesfield & Locks 4 and 5, Bentley Canal
(*Photographs: Railway & Canal Historical Society Weaver Collection Ref 45141 & 45142*)

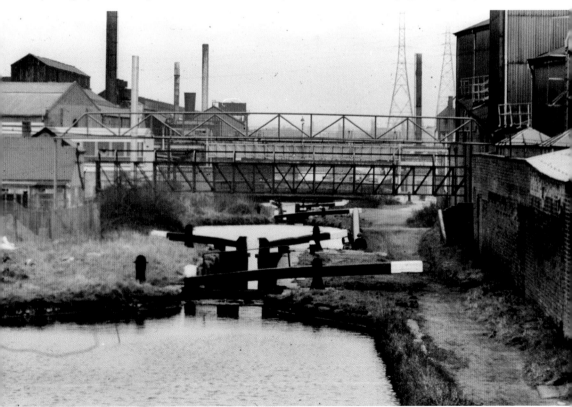

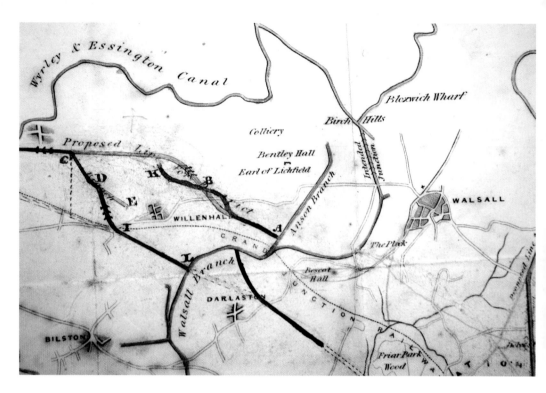

## Canal Maps

The Bentley Canal as built was different to that as originally suggested for the Birmingham Canal Navigations. The upper image shows the original intention of two separate branches and the lower amended plan.

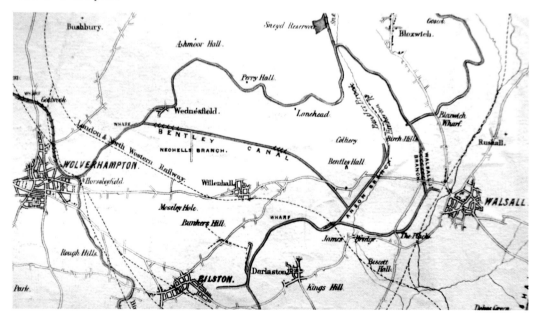

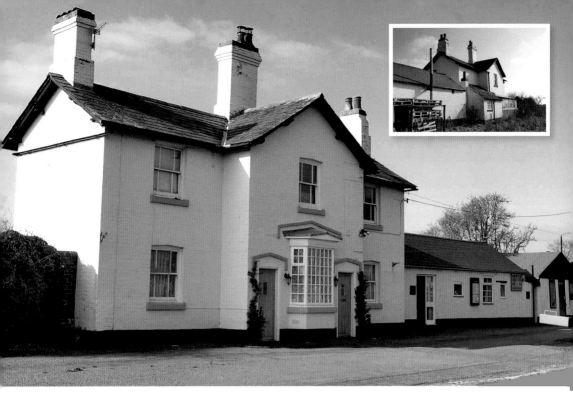

Rushall Top Lock and Cottage & Lock 3 and Lock House, Rushall Canal

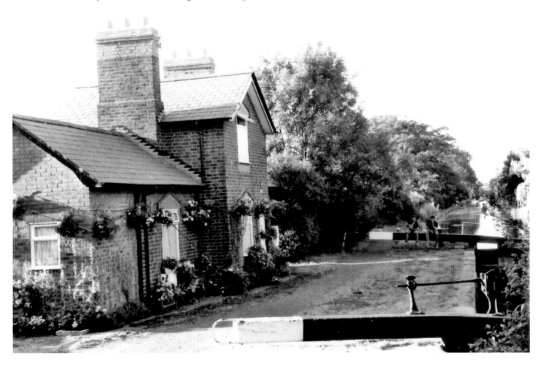

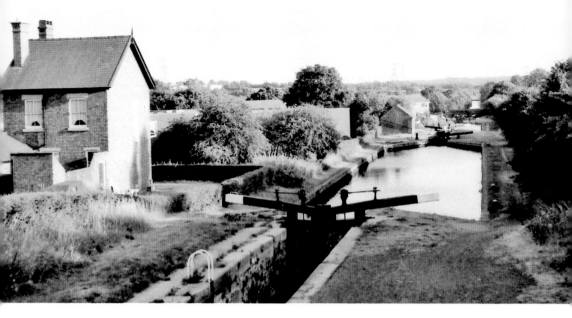

Rushall Locks & Junction of Rushall Canal and the Tame Valley Canal

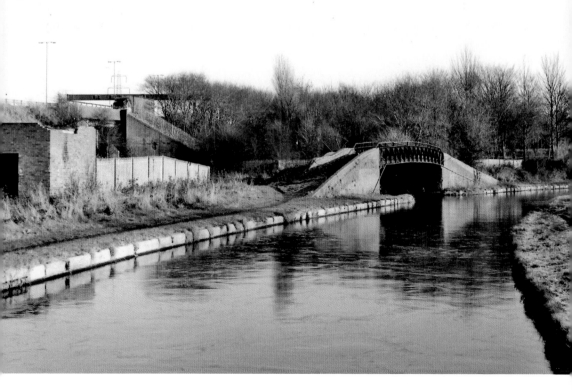

# The Anglesey Branch Canal

The Anglesey Branch was constructed as a canal feeder linking the Cannock Wood Great Reservoir with the Wyrley & Essington Canal at Ogley Hay. This was made as a narrow unnavigable watercourse that involved a tunnel under land near Watling Street.

During September 1849, the Marquis of Anglesey requested that the Cannock Chase feeder be widened and deepened. Work on sinking the Hammerwich Colliery had commenced, or was about to commence, and the Marquis was anxious to send his coals by canal. A standard gauge railway branch was made about the same time to link the pithead with the South Staffordshire Railway.

The feeder was widened and made navigable during 1850 and 1851, chiefly to serve the new Hammerwich Colliery, belonging to the Marquis of Anglesey. During the course of the work the route of the feeder was straightened out and the small reservoir associated with the feeder was taken out of use.

Tenders for widening the feeder were let in sections. John Boys, junior, was given the contract and he carried out the bulk of the work, although some of this work was subsequently sublet to another contractor named Woodhouse, who had also tendered. G. Leatherland also did some culvert work.

BCN inspector (for No. 4 district) James Thomas had prepared three contracts and laid down detailed specifications for contractors to tender. These instructions were extended even to earth excavated for the new cut. Some of the spoil was to be used to fill up hollows and sections of the original feeder. Gravel and stones were to be preserved for 'metalling' the different bridges. All 'rock sand' was to be preserved and deposited near the company's stone shed. He also specified a deadline for the work to be finished. The work had to be finished by 31 May 1850, although after the contract had been finally let, this time limit was perhaps optimistic.

Work had commenced by February 1850. James Thomas reported, in March 1850, that Boys was proceeding sufficiently with the execution of the Anglesey Branch, but the work let to Woodhouse was not being carried out at the desired rapidity. Woodhouse was censured, but managed to improve his work-rate the following week.

In addition to cutting and widening work, a towpath had to be provided. Work on the contract proceeded through 1850 and into 1851. As the work neared completion, an iron bridge was to be put over the canal at Ogley to connect with the Anglesey Branch. This bridge, made by the Horseley Company, had been previously supplied to the Birmingham Canal Navigations at another location (possibly Eyre Street Junction), but was relocated to Ogley when the request for the bridge was made.

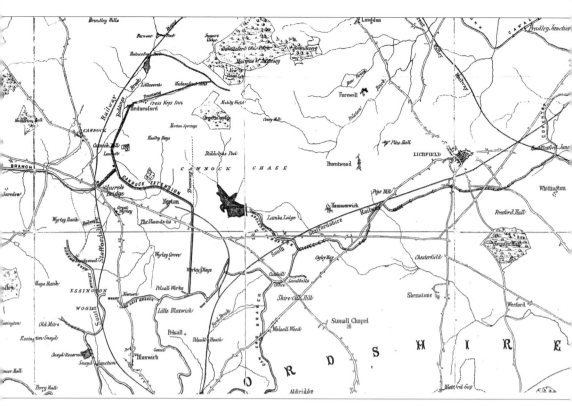

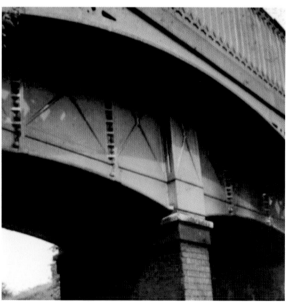

**Northern Extensions & Iron Aqueduct, Anglesey Branch**

New coal mines were established to the north of the Wyrley & Essington Canal and were served by the Wyrley Bank, Cannock Extension and Anglesey Branch. The making of the South Staffordshire Railway line between Wichnor, Lichfield and Walsall (1847–49) involved the diversion of the feeder from Chasewater Reservoir to Ogley and construction of a cast iron aqueduct to carry the water over the railway. Provision was made for this aqueduct to support a navigable canal, which happened when the feeder was converted into the navigable Anglesey Branch (1850/51). (*RCHS, Stuart Chrystal Collection*)

# Cannock Chase Extension Canal

This canal was perhaps the most useful project to bring a waterway link to the deep coal mines being developed on the Chase. The building of this canal provided coal for the industries and households in the Black Country and Birmingham. Built in two stages, the first was completed by Chambers & Hilton as far as Rumer Hill, the rest being finished by BCN workers to complete the canal to Hednesford Basin in 1863. (*Below*) The Extension canal provided waterway access to a number of deep coal mines which were developed during the 1860s and '70s.

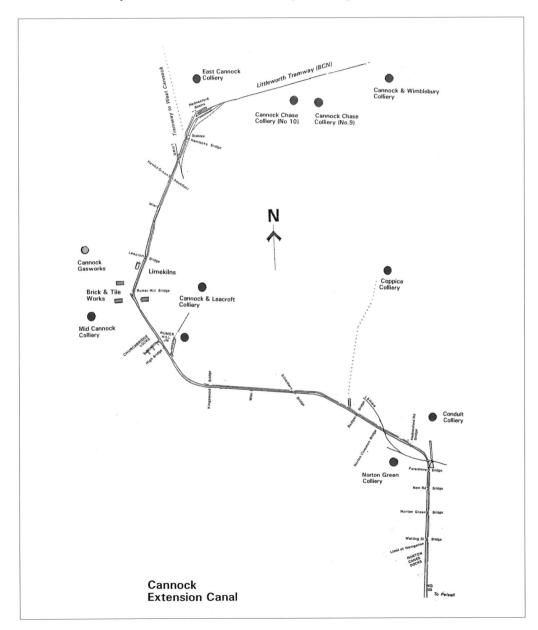

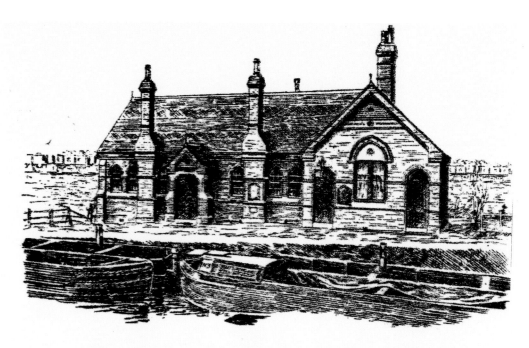

## Boatmen's Hall, Hednesford.

**Boatmen's Mission, Hednesford & Pelsall Stop**

The Victorian concern for religion and education led to the establishment of missions for boatmen at Hednesford and Birchills. The Cannock Extension was seen from Pelsall Stop looking north. The buildings on the left include stables constructed and altered during the first decade of the twentieth century.

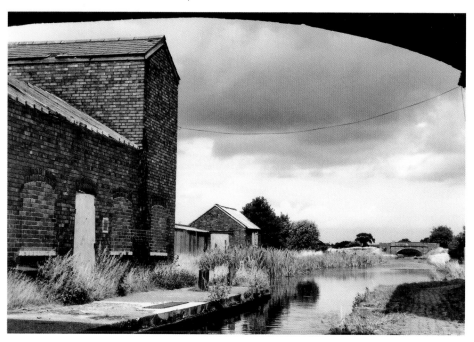

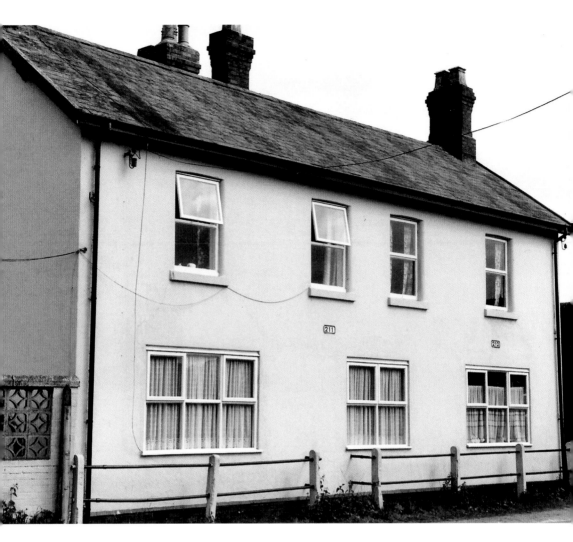

**Canal Cottages, Pelsall**

The Pelsall canal cottages were erected in around 1884. They are placed near the junction with the main Wyrley & Essington Canal. The canal north of here was principally cut through level ground with bridges spanning the canal at intervals. The final section was finished by canal company workers and included an embankment and aqueduct over Hawk's Green Road.

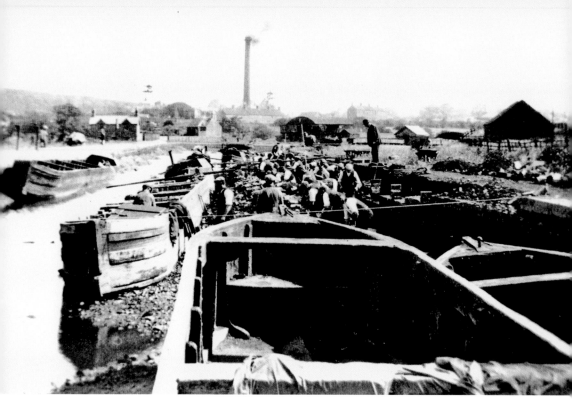

**Cannock Extension Canal, Maintenance Work & Plan of Aqueduct**
In this view of the terminus basin at Hednesford the canal has been drained to assist canal workmen to repair the walls and banks. Mining caused serious subsidence in this location, which eventually caused the canal to be closed.

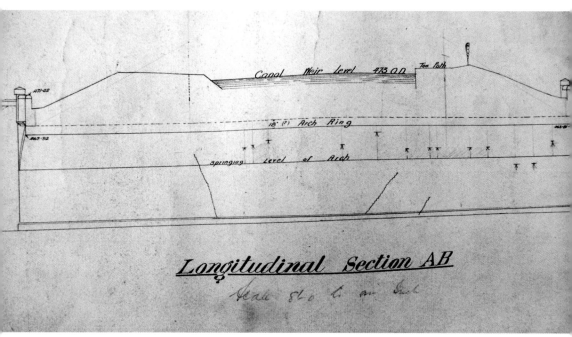

*Longitudinal Section AB*

# Wyrley Bank Canal

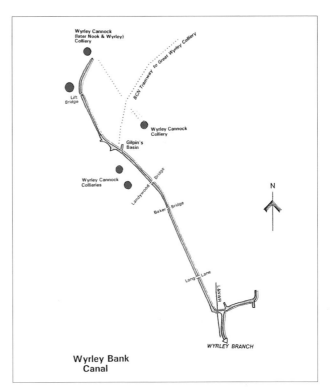

Wyrley Cannock
(later Nook & Wyrley)
Colliery

BCN Tramway to Great Wyrley Colliery

Lift
Bridge

Wyrley Cannock
Colliery

Gilpin's
Basin

Wyrley Cannock
Collieries

Landywood Bridge

Bakers Bridge

Long Lane

L&NWR

WYRLEY BRANCH

N

**Wyrley Bank
Canal**

**Wyrley Bank Canal & Lift
Bridge and Footbridge**
The Wyrley Bank was built by
Chambers & Hilton, linking
the Wyrley Canal with a new
terminus near Cheslyn Hay,
serving a mining area already
reached by a canal tramway
that terminated beside a basin
on the Hatherton Branch Canal.
It enabled new mines to be
established and a BCN tramway
provided a link to the principal
mine at Great Wyrley.

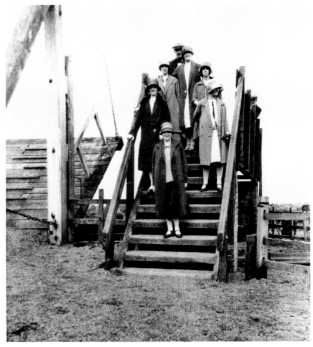

# Norton Springs Branch
# & Littleworth Tramway

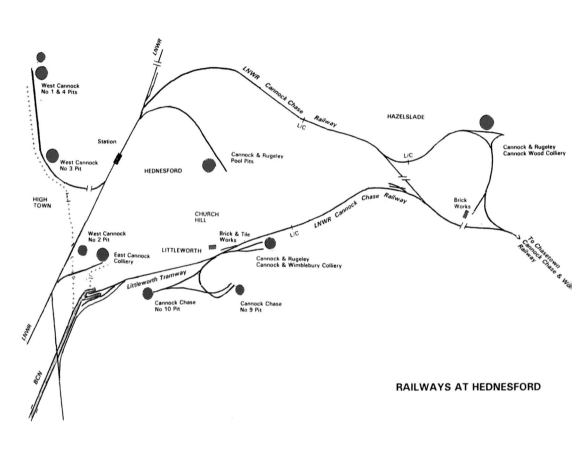

**RAILWAYS AT HEDNESFORD**

Map labels: West Cannock No 1 & 4 Pits, LNWR, LNWR Cannock Chase Railway, HAZELSLADE, L/C, Cannock & Rugeley Cannock Wood Colliery, Station, Cannock & Rugeley Pool Pits, L/C, West Cannock No 3 Pit, HEDNESFORD, HIGH TOWN, CHURCH HILL, LNWR Cannock Chase Railway, L/C, Brick Works, West Cannock No 2 Pit, Brick & Tile Works, L/C, LITTLEWORTH, East Cannock Colliery, Littleworth Tramway, Cannock & Rugeley Cannock & Wimblebury Colliery, To Chasetown Cannock Chase & Wo Railway, Cannock Chase No 10 Pit, Cannock Chase No 9 Pit, LNWR, BCN

### Littleworth Tramway

The Norton Springs Branch was a short branch built to serve the mines at Conuit Colliery. The Birmingham Canal Navigations was connected to Hednesford Colliery by a canal company tramway when the Cannock Extension was completed to Hednesford Basin. This tramway was standard gauge and joined up with the London & Western Railway Cannock Chase Branch and also the private Cannock Chase & Wolverhampton Railway (which served the Cannock Chase Colliery Company pits 1–8). The Littleworth Tramway served Cannock Chase pits 9 and 10 (formerly Hednesford Colliery) and the Cannock & Wimblebury Colliery. The Hednesford Railway Network is seen above.

Chapter Four

# New Trade & Industry

The making of the additional links between the Birmingham Canal and the Wyrley & Essington proved to be an important incentive to businesses on the route of the Wyrley & Essington. Various trades were served by the canal: brickmaking; boatbuilding; bone trade; chemical trade; engineering; flour milling; gasworks; iron making; iron foundry; paint and varnish; sand; and water.

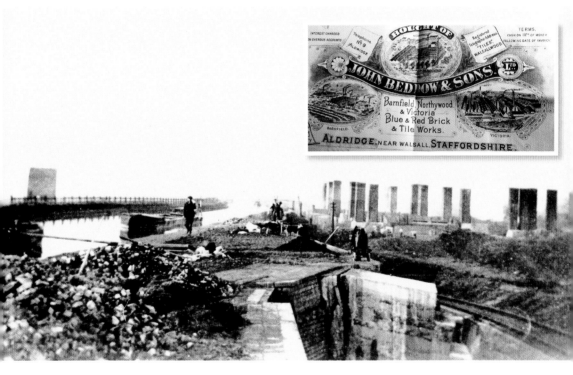

**Brickworks on the Daw End Branch, Near Aldridge**
The brick industry is still conducted near Aldridge. Local clays were utilised to make bricks at several canal-side kilns. Coal was required for heating the kilns and in this view coal is stacked alongside the waterway, ready to be taken by brickyard tramway to the works. The inset shows the Letter Head for Barnett's Brickworks, Aldridge.

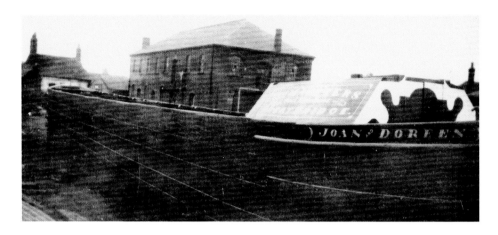

## Boatbuilding at Pratt's Bridge & Boatbuilding, Ken Keay

A feature of the canals around Birmingham and the Black Country was the boatbuilding business. It was a business that was divided into essentially two categories: iron boats and wooden boats. A facet of iron boatbuilding was the requirement to join the metal parts by rivets, and this type of boatbuilding was carried on by a select group of builders. A more general trade was wooden boatbuilding, and several boatyards were located beside the Wyrley & Essington and connecting waterways. In this 1930s view, the *Joan & Doreen* is seen at Peter Keay's Boatyard, Pratt's Bridge, Bloxwich. This yard was located at what was called Bloxwich Wharf. There was a basin here that had been the terminus of the tramway from limestone quarries and also may have served as an early carrier's depot. The Pratt family were millers at the steam mill here at one time and gave their name to the bridge that carried the turnpike over the canal.

Ken Keay carried on the boatbuilding skills of his father. Before his death Ken produced a detailed set of drawings that detailed his boatbuilding life. These drawings included representations of the yards Peter Keay had at Daw Ends and Bloxwich. There were also sketches to show how wooden boats were put together. A careful choice of wood, working and shaping were needed to complete a wooden narrowboat or repair it. (*Below drawing: Edward Paget, Tomlinson Collection*)

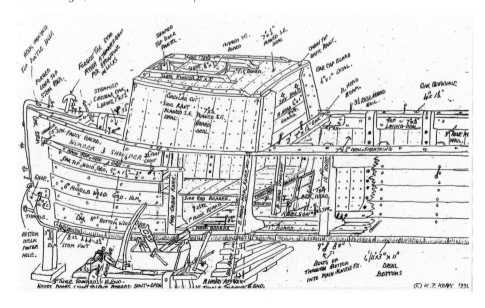

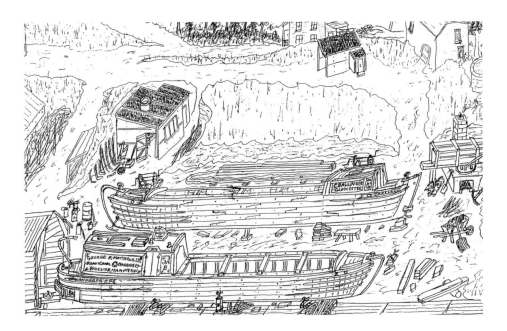

### Boatbuilding at Daw End & Carl Street Boatyard, Bloxwich, 1983

Boatyards were simply plots of land beside the canal where there was sufficient space to erect boats on the bank. Some yards had covering sheds to enable the builder to work under shelter. That at Daw End evidently had moveable shelter (*far left*). Ken Keay also included a steam chest in this sketch (*far right*) where timber was bent into shape using steam to render the wood pliable. Carl Street boatyard was placed west of Pratt's Bridge. It was occupied by various boatbuilders, but during the twentieth century the occupier was Worsey's, who owned several yards to repair wooden boats and build new wooden narrowboats. Peter Keay later owned this yard and his son, Ken, was the last boatbuilder there. The view shows the abandoned yard and the remnants of boats. The offside length has a number of boat hulls. (*Above drawing: Edward Paget, Tomlinson Collection*)

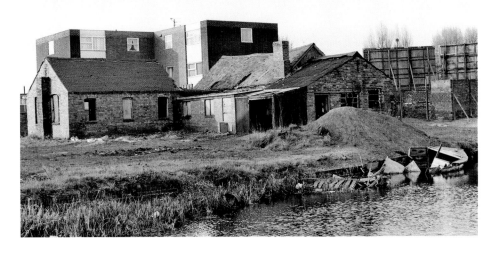

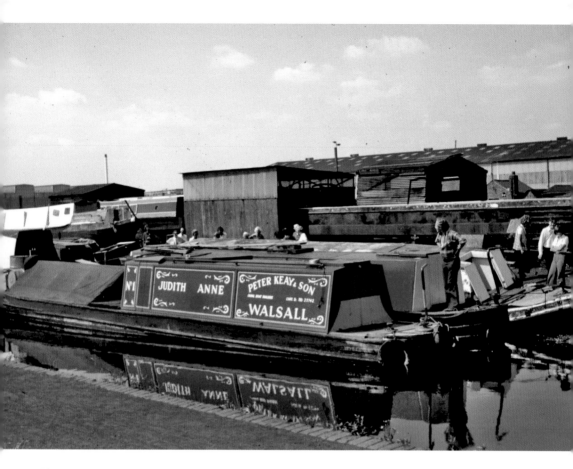

## Ken Keay

Ken Keay, like other boatbuilders of his time, would convert former working boats for pleasure use, as seen in the inset showing the tug *Judith Ann* and a former working boat on the dock undergoing conversion. One process was to take a 70-foot narrowboat and cut it into two, creating one or two boats for boaters to purchase and use for cruising. For the dedicated boat historian it was a process that made tracing the future history of the craft difficult, but for the boater it ensured a continued and useful life for the craft, even if it was for non-commercial purposes.

The historian Laurence Hogg has made some observations about the boats in Ken Keay boatyard view. 'It shows *Judith Ann*, the dock and the stern of what may be *Chalfront*. Alongside, with the white cabin, is the *Silver Jubilee*. Ahead of the *Judith Ann* could be *Kew* and to the right is Selwyns hire boat *Lady Helen*. The butty in the dock remains unidentified, while the metal hull on the bank was a former *Bantock* craft.' (*Photograph: Chris Bartlett*)

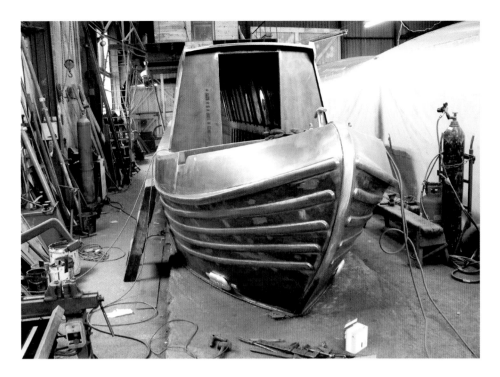

**Boat Construction at Canal Boat Services**
A narrowboat body shell is assembled indoors. The almost clinical and ordered scene is a remarkable contrast to boatbuilding in former times, which was often conducted outdoors alongside the canal bank. (*Below*) The Cannock Extension Canal now terminates south of the A5 (Watling Street) and near this terminus is the base of Canal Boat Services, which is a family owned business, where the Cooper family build, repair and paint narrowboats for the boating trade. The tug *Entreprise*, which was at one time used by Ernie Thomas to haul coal to Brichills Power Station, is seen outside the boatyard after a repaint. (*Matt Cooper, Canal Boat Sevices*)

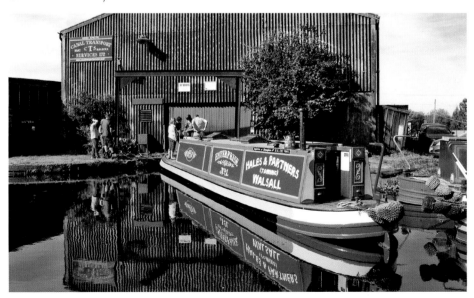

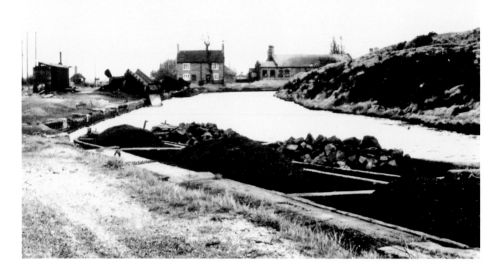

### Anglesey Basin & Walsall Wood Colliery, Daw End Canal

The first of the Cannock Chase collieries were served by the Anglesey Branch. The feeder from Cannock Chase Reservoir had been made navigable between 1850 and 1851 to receive coal from the coal mines belonging to the Earl of Anglesey. It remained a regular supplier of coal from the mines until the National Coal Board chose to close the mines that served it in 1962. Coal was still brought by lorry from the mines still at work and tipped onto the chutes and into the holds of boats.

The deep coal mines were frequent skyline features, where the colliery screens and pit-heads were also accompanied by tall spoil heaps. The inset shows the Walsall Wood Colliery pit-head, 1954, which was served by railway sidings that linked both with the former Midland Railway Brownhills Branch and a branch railway to the former LNWR/South Staffordshire Railway near Pelsall. (*Author's collection, courtesy late E. E. Pritchard*)

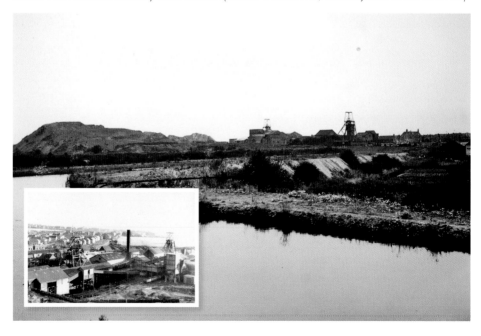

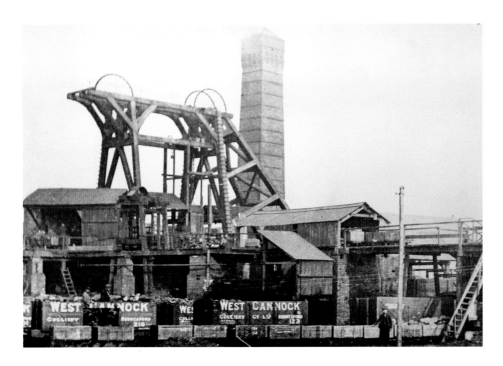

### West Cannock Colliery & Cannock Extension Canal, Hednesford Basin

The pit-head and screens was a congested site at this pit with pit tub tramways on two levels. The lower pit tub track was used to convey coal to a loading staithe at Hednesford Basin. The colliery company possessed its own locomotives and rail wagons and these wagons were taken down to the exchange sidings at Hednesford.

The Littleworth Tramway was a standard gauge railway that linked the canal terminus basins at Hednesford with other freight lines. The Cannock & Rugeley Colliery Company and the Cannock Chase Colliery Company both were able to bring loaded coal wagons down to the wharf for loading coal into boats. In this NCB-period view, former Cannock & Rugeley Colliery Company locomotive *Rawnsley* stands at the head of a train of coal boxes, which are lifted off individually from the wagon base for tipping coal into the hold of boats in the adjacent basin. (*Author's collection, courtesy late E. E. Pritchard*)

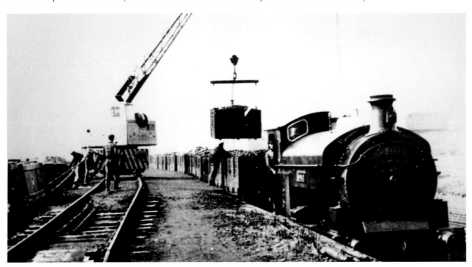

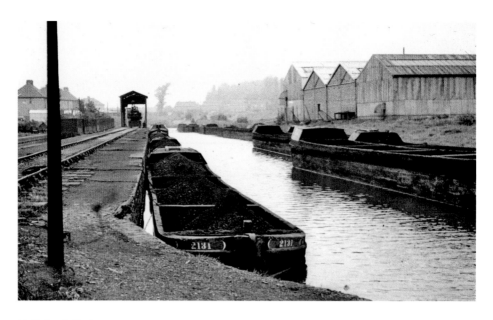

### Hollybank Basin

The power stations at Wolverhampton and Birchills both were located beside the 473-foot level, and the regular traffic in coal for the power station boilers and the mines on Cannock Chase or Essington could be towed along the waterway without passing through a single lock. Hollybank Basin remained a busy wharf for coal supplies to the power stations. In this 1960s view, loaded boats destined for local power stations await a tug to haul to the power station.

Another view of the basin, which shows the specially built coal-boxes and railway wagons that carried coal from the Hilton Main Colliery to Hollybank Basin. The rail crane was employed to transfer the coal boxes between wagon and boat. These boxes released their contents into the hold of the boat and the empty boxes were returned to the wagon bogie. (*Railway & Canal Historical Society Weaver Collection Ref 45542 & 45543*)

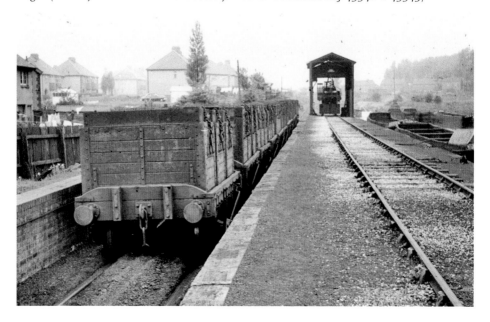

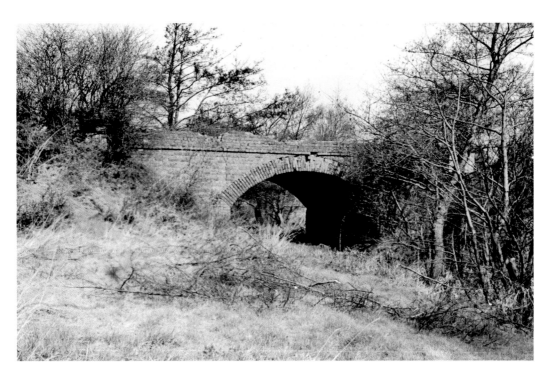

## Coppice Colliery Basin & Grove Colliery Basin, Cannock Extension Canal

The Coppice Colliery, Heath Hayes, was opened during 1894. Coal went out by rail along the LNWR Five Ways Branch or was conveyed along a rope-worked tramway to Coppice Colliery Basin beside the Cannock Extension Canal at Norton Canes. This basin was both wide and long and enabled pit tubs to be unloaded and the coal shovelled into the hold of the boat alongside.
(*Above photograph: Railway & Canal Historical Society Weaver Collection Ref 45253*)

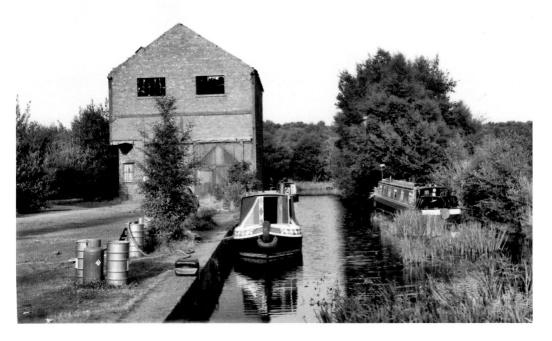

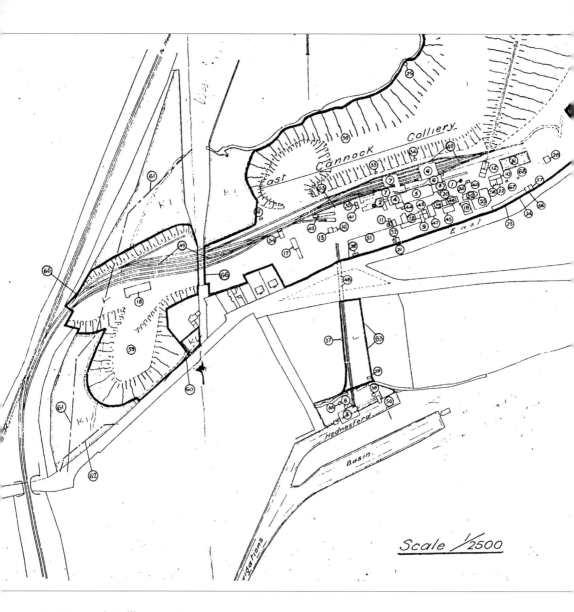

**East Cannock Colliery, 1946**

This plan was produced at the time collieries passed from private ownership to the National Coal Board. Among the features numbered, the tramway to the canal basin is of relevance to the trade that passed that way. The two shafts, (1) the No. 1 Shaft and (2) the No. 2 Shaft, are associated with the railway-served screening plant – (6) No. 1 Screen & (7) No. 2 Screen. The canal loading wharf (50) also had a separate screening plant (8).

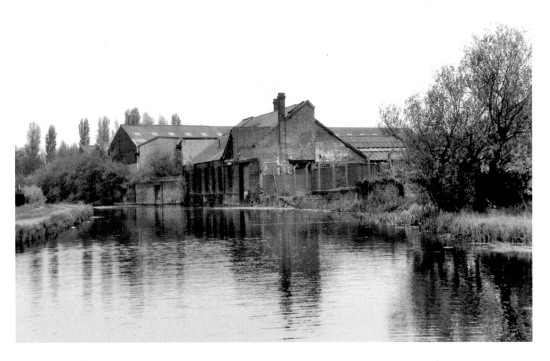

**Edward's Edge Tool Factory, Wednesfield, 1994 & 2011**
Edward's first established an edge tool factory at Horseley Fields on the site of Union Wharf (a former carrier's wharf that belonged to Crowley & Co.), which became known as the Griffin Works. The new factory at Wednesfield was opened as Edward's business increased and became known as the New Griffin Works.

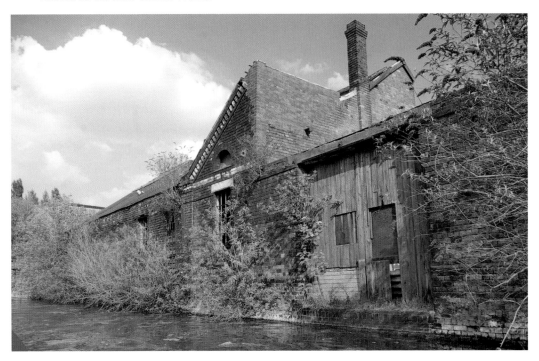

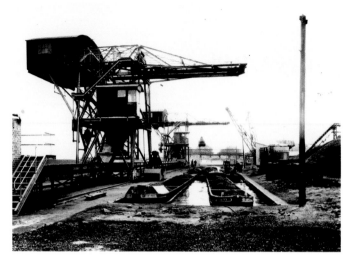

Birchills Power Station, B Power Station Wharf & Water Supply, 1923 The original basin was enlarged and equipped with modern telphers to collect the coal from the boats and transfer it to the No. 8 coal conveyor for the power station. The boats were owned by the power authority, which was ultimately the Central Electricity Generating Board. Ernie Thomas hauled trains of these boats from the collieries using tugs, such as the *Enterprise*. The traffic to Birchills Power Station ceased activity in May 1965. Birchills Power Station drew water from the Anson Branch. A pumping station raised water for cooling purposes to the power station and was returned to the Birchills Branch after use.

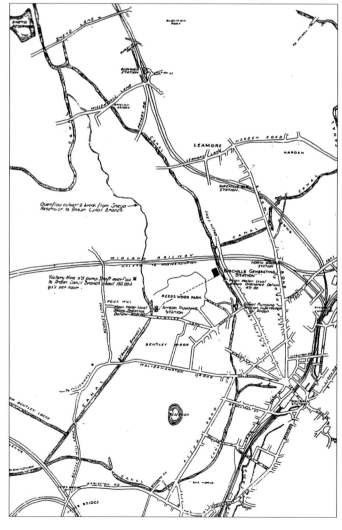

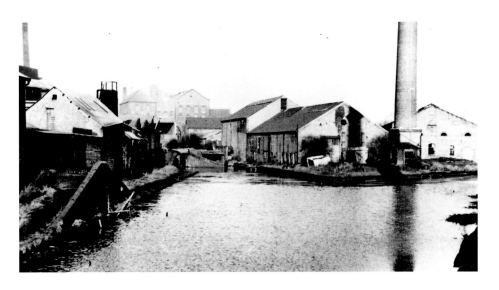

Walsall's First Power Station Site & Advertisement for Lime

(*Above*) The Walsall Junction Canal joined the Birmingham Canal Navigations' Walsall Canal. It was completed during 1841 and provided a link between the Wyrley & Essington and the Birmingham. The Walsall Canal, which continued on to the Park Street terminus, was lined with industry and wharves. During the early decades of the nineteenth century, there were extensive limestone wharves and mines placed on the land between the two canals. With their closure the property was converted for other uses. Walsall Corporation built a gasworks there, whose retort house (with the sunburst-style windows) remained for many years. After the corporation built a new gasworks at the Pleck, the gasworks was converted into a station to generate electricity and boats loaded with coal would line the canal side here. Electricity generation ceased after a new power station was opened above the locks at Birchills.

(*Below*) Aris's Gazette (July 1807) published this advertisement from the owners of Daw End & Moss Close Limeworks that included canal carriage to other local destinations.

## LIME.

MESSRS. FEREDAY, TURTON, and PARSON beg Leave to inform their Friends and the Public, that there will be a regular Supply of the beſt white Lime, at the following Works, at the Prices ſpecified underneath :—

|  | | s. | D. |
|---|---|---|---|
| Daw End | — — | 11 | 6 | per Ton |
| Mofs Cloſe | — — | 11 | 6 | ditto |
| Catſhill | — — | 12 | 6 | ditto |
| Aldridge | — — | 12 | 8 | ditto |
| Eſſington | — — | 13 | 0 | ditto |
| Lichfield | — — | 14 | 6 | ditto |

Provided the Accounts are paid regularly on the Quarter Day ſucceeding the Delivery, an Allowance of 1s. 6d. per Ton will be deducted; *but on no Account whatever will the Allowance be taken off, unleſs paid as above.*
Ruſhall Hall, June 10, 1807.

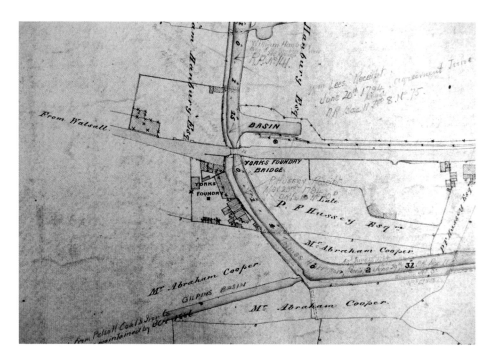

**Yorks Foundry, Cotterrill's Map of Wyrley & Essington, 1868 & Ogley Lock, 1–4, 1868**
(*Above*) There were three foundries in the Pelsall area – Goscote, Pelsall and Yorks – that supplied engineering parts for the steam-driven plant located on the South Staffordshire & Cannock Chase Coalfield. (*Below*) Cotterrill's map of the Wyrley & Essington Canal produced in 1868 shows the former workshop buildings that were once located there. These premises engaged in lock gate construction and carpentry work and there was also a boat dock placed below Lock 2 that evidently could be drained into the pounds below Lock 3. The red crosses show that these structures were later taken down. This alteration happened after the new depot at Sneyd was constructed.

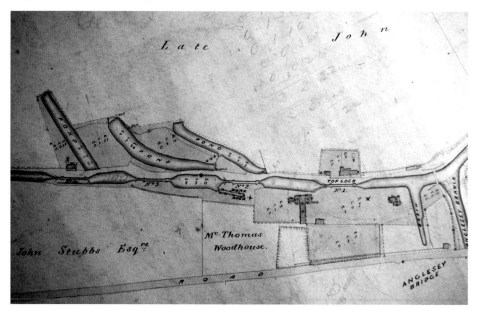

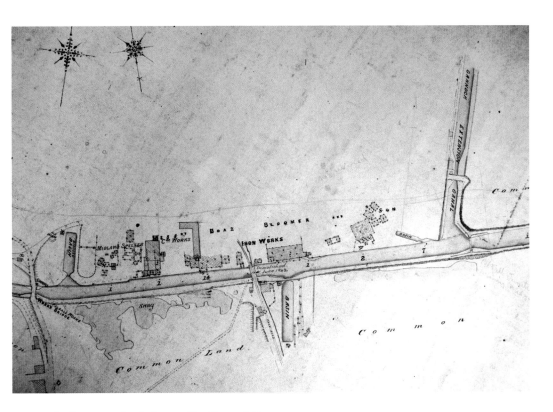

## Pelsall Ironworks & Cotterrill's Map, 1868

In this view the full canal frontage is seen. From left to right the first structures are the two iron-cased blast furnaces and incline, then there are three separate ironworks each with rolling mills and puddling furnaces and canal warehouses. The overbridge, far right, carried the standard gauge railway from the LNWR exchange sidings to the ironworks and associated collieries. The ironworks were spread out along the offside of the canal. They closed during 1891 and were dismantled from 1892. The railway was kept open for colliery traffic until around 1903 and later for slag removal. The site of the later Midland Spelter Works is also recorded on this map.

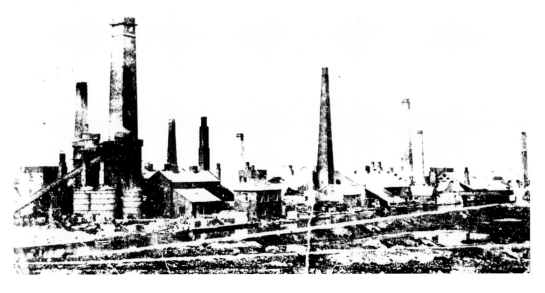

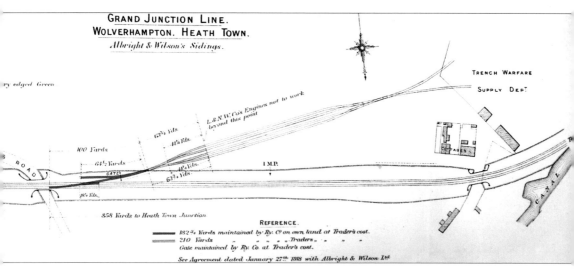

GRAND JUNCTION LINE.
WOLVERHAMPTON. HEATH TOWN.
*Albright & Wilson's Sidings.*

REFERENCE.

━━━━ 182¾ Yards maintained by Ry. C° on own land at Trader's cost.
═══ 210 Yards    „    „    „    „ Trader's „    „    „
Gate maintained by Ry. C°. at Trader's cost.

*See Agreement dated January 27th 1918 with Albright & Wilson Ltd.*

**Heath Town and Wilson's Depot & Mander's Paint Factory, Wednesfield, 1994**
During the First World War, a munitions factory was established at Heath Town, Wolverhampton, beside the canal. This factory was managed by Albright & Wilson, who provided phosphorus for the Trench Warfare Supply Depot. After the war, Ministry of Munitions Wolverhampton was sold and the buildings adapted by Mander Brothers for paint manufacture. Mander Bros were a long-established varnish and paint manufacturer who took over the former ammunition factory during the 1920s.

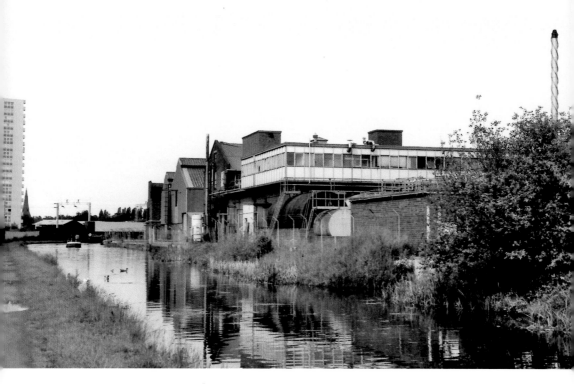

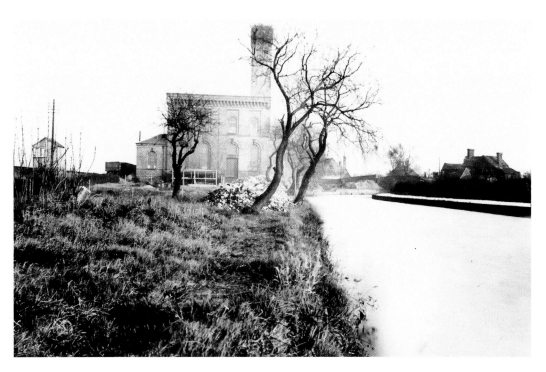

**South Staffordshire Water Co., Sandfields Pumping Station**
The original pumping establishment comprised two engine houses; one held the original pumping plant, the other the G. & J. Davis engine. (*Below*) The new waterworks extensions (*c.* 1930) and the G. & J. engine house.

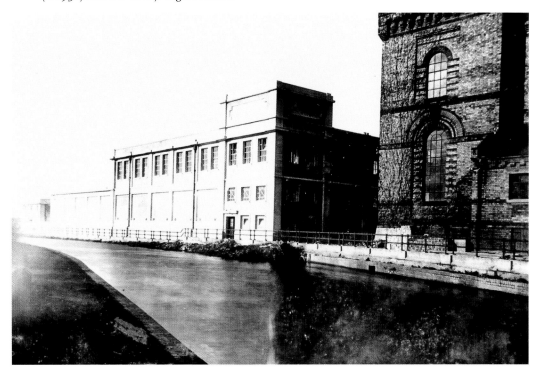

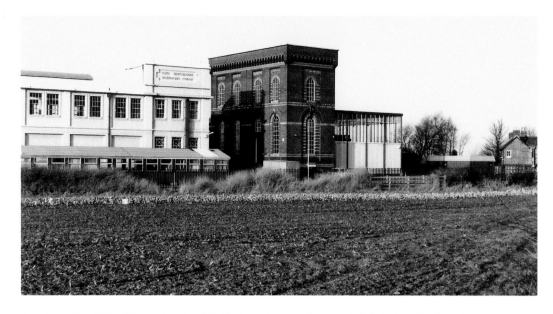

**South Staffordshire Water Co., Sandfields Pumping Station, 1998 & Price's Mill, Bloxwich, 1934**
*(Above)* The route of the Wyrley & Essington Canal passed along the foreground of the waterworks buildings. *(Below)* The flour mill at Bloxwich was initially owned by the Pratt family, who were associated with various Midland flour mills. Later this mill became known as Price's Mill. Corn was brought to the mill by Shropshire Union Railway & Canal carrying boats and when this company ceased trading, the trade was taken over by the Midland & Coast Canal Carrying Company. A Midland & Coast narrowboat, *Taurus*, is shown here moored alongside the mill. *(Below photograph: Walsall Archives)*

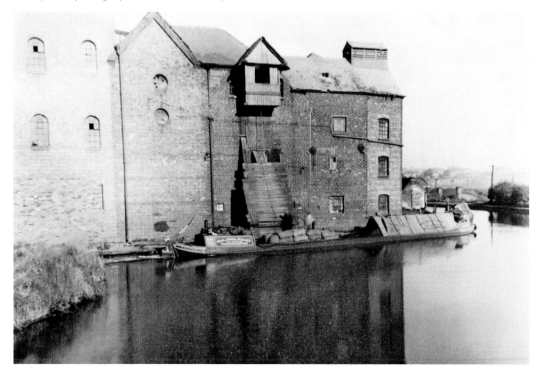

# Working Boats

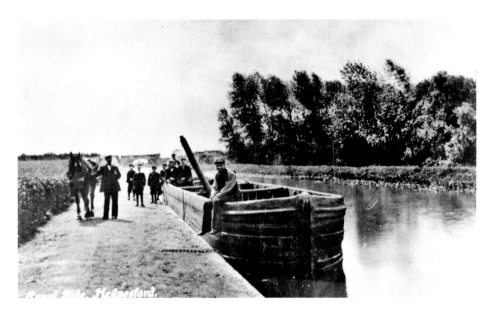

**Narrowboat and Horse Near Hednesford & Narrowboats at Pinfolds Bridge**
(*Above*) An open narrowboat moored alongside the Cannock Extension Canal near Hednesford. (*Below*) Three coal-laden boats were photographed and evidently carefully posed for this shot. It is likely that these boats were *en route* to Wolverhampton Power Station and may have either been loaded at Hollybank or Hednesford. The method of tipping from rail-borne coal boxes into the boat hold led to heaps of coal in the hold, which was a concern to some boatmen as the heavy, unequal weight meant that the boat dragged along the bottom of the canal. (*Above photograph: Railway & Canal Historical Society Ref 65997*)

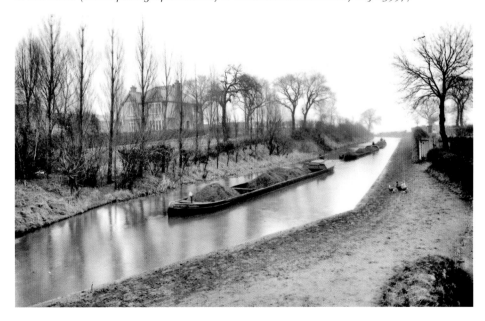

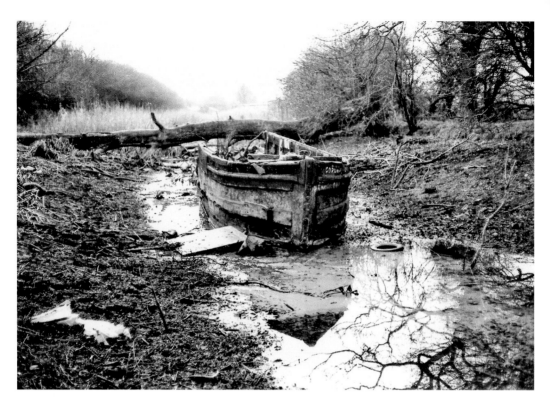

*Coronation* Broken Up Near Huddlesford, 1970 & Cannock Extension Canal, Norton Canes
(*Above*) When traffic ceased from the mines, boats were abandoned alongside the line of canals
such as the Cannock Extension. *Coronation* met its fate a few years earlier when the canal was
shut from Ogley to Huddlesford. The broken shell of this former coal boat was seen on the bed
of the canal some fifteen years after the canal had closed. (*Below*) Tug and loaded butties on tow
from the mines on the Cannock Extension Canal heading towards Pelsall.

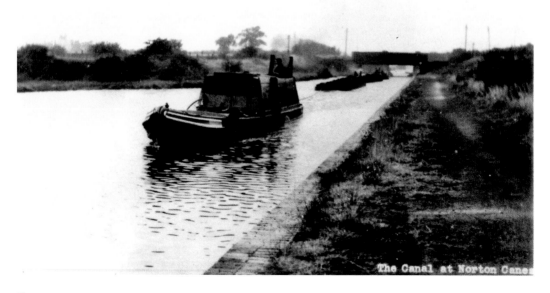

The Canal at Norton Canes

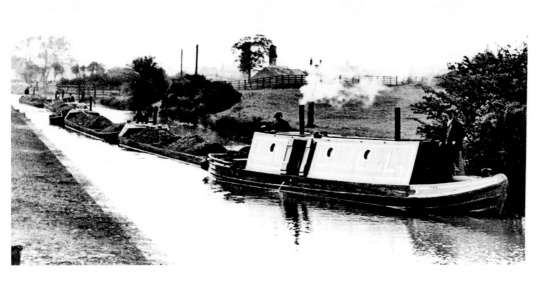

**Leonard Leigh Tug *Joan II* & Mitchard's Tug at Pratt's Mill, Bloxwich**

(*Above*) *Joan II* is seen towing a train of boats. (*Below*) Coal merchants such as Mitchard of Tipton, would fetch coal from the Cannock Chase collieries for their business. Their tug *Jubilee* hauled a train of boats behind it. Among Mitchard's fleet of boats were the longer and wider narrowboat known as the Hampton Boat, which could not pass a lock but could work between the collieries, Wolverhampton and the top of the locks at Tipton. (*Above photograph: Black Country Museum. Below photograph: Walsall Archives*)

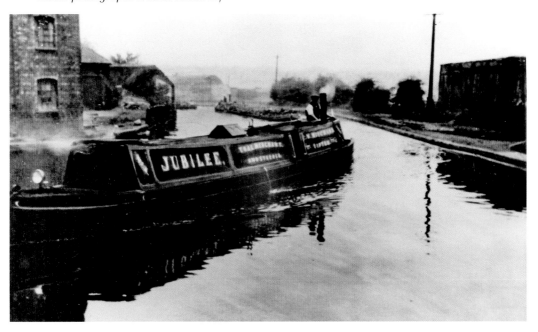

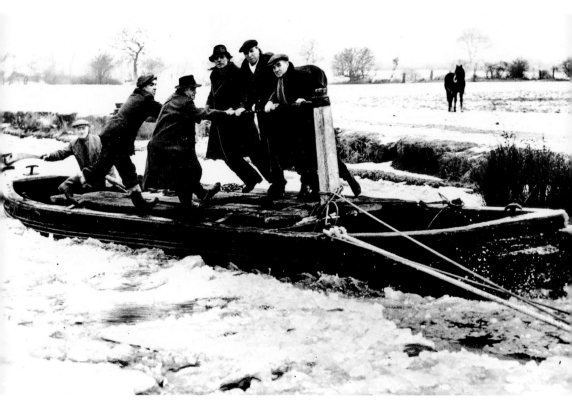

**Iceboat *Ross***

The Birmingham Canal Navigations had a number of iceboats so as to keep the navigation open during the coldest weather. The Wyrley & Essington Canal and the branches to the Cannock Chase collieries had long and exposed sections that were particularly vulnerable to blockage by ice. The Walsall, or No. 4, district had up to six wooden or iron iceboats assigned to it to maintain an open navigation. The *Ross* was an iron boat.

# Chapter Five

# Canal Infrastructure

Every canal undertaking has its share of structures and features. All structures are dictated by the terrain, through which the canal passes, and the skills of the engineer who planned the route. Although finance and hostile landowners also contribute to the mix, the final result is a unique synthesis that is specific for each waterway. Some might incorporate all that is bad; others are credited as basically good. Most have some bad points.

The construction of the Wyrley & Essington Canal was better fated than most. The only major problem, it seems, was the collapse of Sneyd Reservoir dam and the damage to the uncompleted Cannock Reservoir dam, both in the summer of 1799. If this state of affairs was due to the skill of the engineer, William Pitt, and the contractor, John Brawn, it is perhaps a credit to their previous experience. Yet even on the Wyrley Canal there were moments where mistakes had to be rectified, but they were not on the scale of other engineering projects. Contemporary contractors such as the Dadfords, Sheasbys and Pinkertons all faced gruelling challenges on their respective contracts, and not all were completed satisfactorily.

The main features on the Wyrley Canal were locks, bridges, cuttings, embankments and reservoirs. Aqueducts were restricted to the odd crossing of a narrow stream and there were no tunnels. There was an embankment at Wednesfield and a deep cutting at Catshill, but generally the main line followed the contours at the 473-foot level, before descending by the thirty locks at Ogley to the Coventry Canal.

One important feature was the Pipe Hill embankment. Today this is still an important structure, even though it has not seen a boat since the early 1950s. This embankment crosses a valley at Pipe Hill and was probably made from earth boated in from deep cutting works, such as existed at Catshill.

Ogley Locks themselves remain the single most important engineering feature on the line. They are spread out over the 7-mile section in groups or singly. The first flight at Ogley Junction comprises eight locks, most of which have long side pounds for the conservation of water. There is then a level section to Muckley Corner, where there is a second flight of four locks. At Fosseway there is a third flight, where there are six locks close together. The locks are then formed singly through Lichfield to St John's Bridge. From Cricket Lane is another flight of four locks to Freeford Bridge. The remaining three locks are then spread out along the line to Huddlesford.

While the Birmingham Canal Navigations improved and repaired structures along the route, there were other external factors. Road widening led to bridge reconstruction. Railway construction also added features to the systems, such as overbridges made of brick or iron.

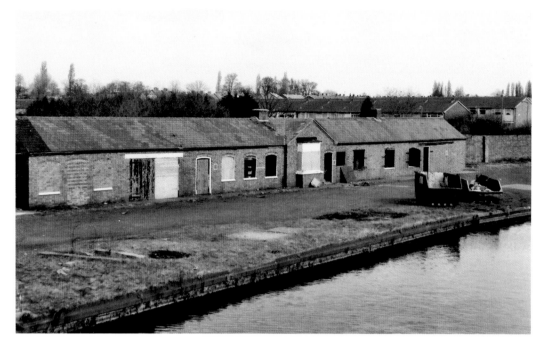

**Sneyd Workshop, Sneyd Junction & Midland Railway Bridge, Brownhills**

The workshops at Sneyd were constructed by the Birmingham Canal Navigations and included stables and later had a part allocated for stores to supply the No. 4 (Walsall District). The iron bridge is similar to other railway bridges in the region, supplied by the Bilston Foundry of Thomas Perry. It carried the Midland Railway, Walsall Wood Branch, over the Wyrley & Essington Canal near Brownhills.

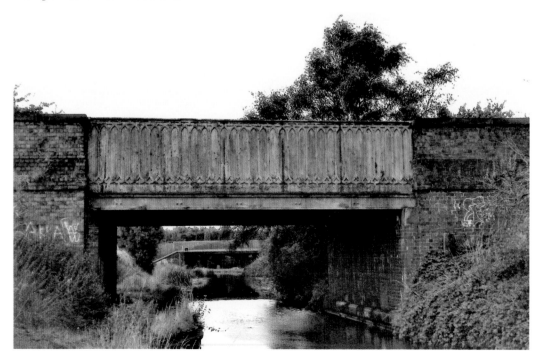

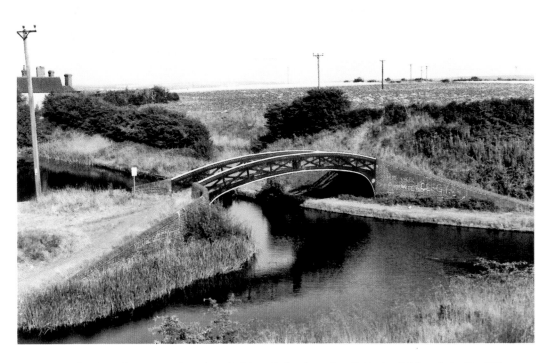

**Horseley Iron Company, Cast Iron Bridge, Ogley Junction & Yorks Bridge, Rebuilt 1866**
(*Above*) This bridge was probably moved from another BCN location. The Anglesey Branch was not completed until 1851. (*Below*) The bridge over the canal at Pelsall was rebuilt in 1866. BCN engineer's minutes record in November that workmen took down the old arch at 'York House Bridge' and rebuilt a new one.

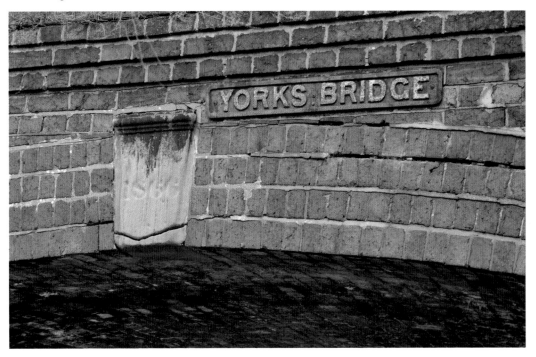

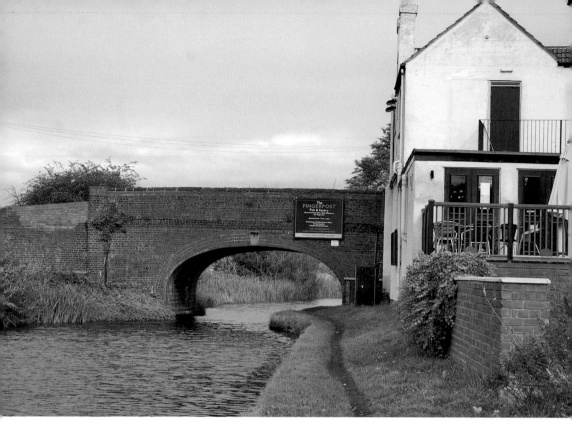

Yorks Bridge, Rebuilt 1866 & Pinfold Bridge, Wednesfield

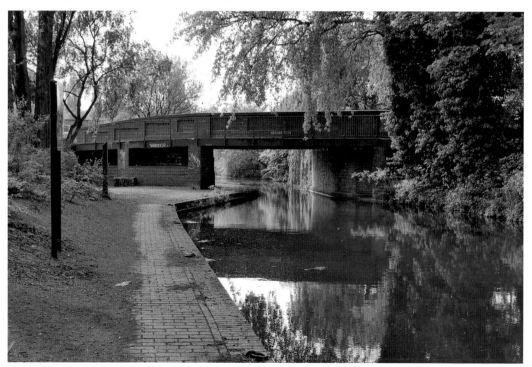

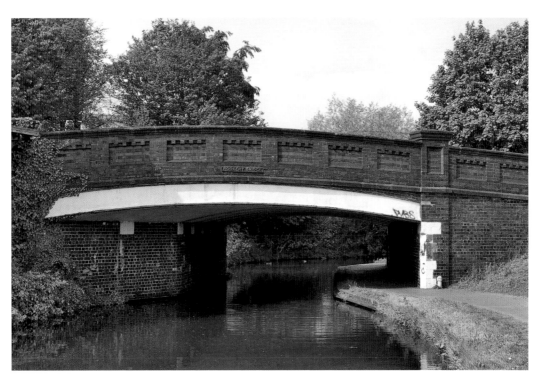

**Rookery Bridge, Wednesfield & Midland Railway Aqueduct, 2011**
Joseph Firbank was the contractor for making the Midland Railway Company line from Water Orton through Aldridge to Walsall. Completed during 1878, this railway work involved a deep cutting near Daw End and the making of a brick aqueduct over the railway. Rookery Bridge belonged to a group of bridges rebuilt for Wolverhampton Corporation road improvement and widening. It comprises a metal span and brick infrastructure.

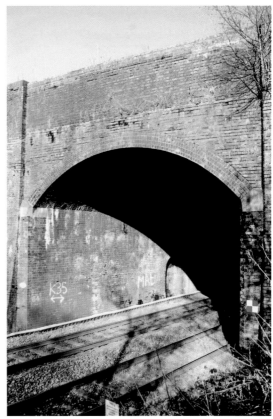

# Chapter Six

# Restoration Schemes

Since the closure of the Ogley Flight in 1954, most locks have been buried. Yet they are a hidden time capsule, still containing the information of how they might have been made. Most, if not all, of these locks were rebuilt by the Birmingham Canal Navigations during the period 1843–50. The present structures have elements of both the original locks and the BCN reconstruction. During the rebuilding work, the lock walls were frequently taken down and faced with blue engineering bricks. The bottoms have generally been left intact and still comprise the red, handmade bricks manufactured during Brawn's time. Lock reconstruction also led to the replacement of the bypass weirs, but some original bypass weirs remain. One has recently been excavated at Lock 24.

Less can be said about the Sneyd Locks, but two are still visible at the junction with the main canal at Bloxwich. The sites of the other three are now partly buried below a roadway. These predate the Ogley Locks and comprise, if the stop lock at Horseley Fields is ignored, the first locks built by Brawn on the Wyrley Canal.

The two reservoirs also rank as important surviving structures. Both were enlarged by the BCN and now occupy a greater area. The levels at Sneyd have been reduced in recent times, but there is still water in the reservoir. Cannock Chase Reservoir remains an important supplier of water to the canal system. The dam has been raised, but hidden under the present structure should be the original dam as constructed by Dadford.

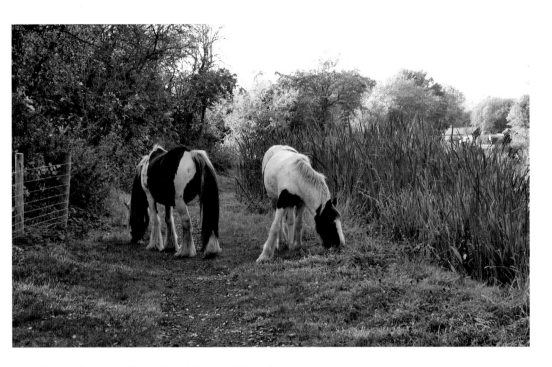

### Towpath Scene, Near Sneyd & Pelsall Junction

British Waterways have made many improvements to the towpath in many places. Unfortunately, fencing is sometimes vandalised. While horses were no stranger to the towpath in the past, hauling boats along the 'cut', in modern times they are rarer visitors, this pair having strayed from the normal grazing onto the towpath through a broken-down fence.

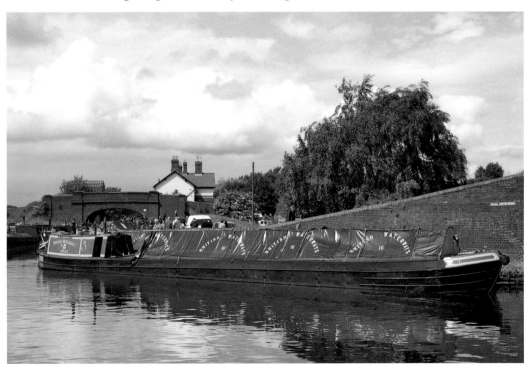

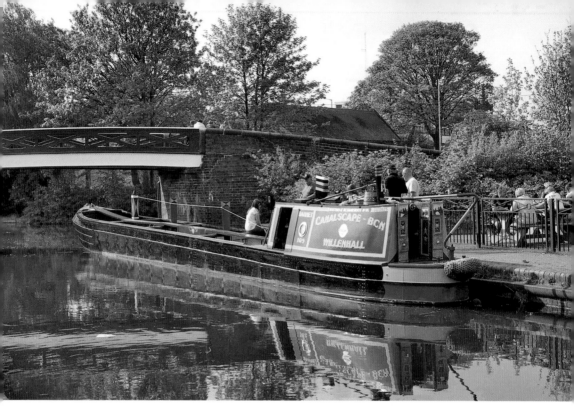

NB *Barnet* at New Cross on the Bentley Canal & Boat Rally at the End of the Anglesey Branch

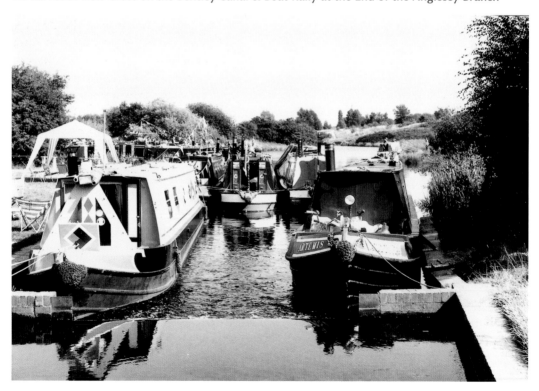

# Lichfield & Hatherton
## Canals Restorations Trust

The Lichfield & Hatherton Canals Trust (LHCT) was set up to restore two disused canals and construct a new link that would encourage navigation on the northern part of the Birmingham Canal Navigations. Commercial carrying in this part of the British canal system fell into decline during the 1950s and had practically ceased after 1964. Various factors contributed to this final decline. The main factor was the exhaustion of the coal measures worked for profitable mining at many of the canal-served collieries. Another factor was the bad winter of 1962/63, when the canal froze and the coal boats were unable to move. Every effort to break the ice was followed by further freezing. Finally there was no water left in the bed of the canal, only ice! The carriage of coal was rerouted to the roads, and that is where it stayed. The remaining coal was taken out of the pits by rail or road. Some coal was delivered by road to chutes at Anglesey Basin and a small canal trade was continued from there until 1970. British Waterways conceded defeat in their battle with subsidence along the Cannock Extension Canal and closed the section north of Watling Street. The southern Cannock Extension remained open to serve Grove Colliery, until this mine closed in June 1963.

The trust intends to restore both the Hatherton Branch (Staffordshire & Worcestershire Canal) and the Ogley Lock Flight of the Birmingham Canal Navigations, and create a new link from the Hatherton Canal through to Grove Colliery Basin.

Restoration work has been conducted at three lock sites along Ogley Locks: Nos 18, 25 and 26. Work is currently proceeding with Lock 26. From Cricket Lane to the Tamworth Road Bridge there were four locks, Nos 24–27. Three of them, 24, 25 and 26, were placed close together. After the canal was abandoned, the bed of the canal still functioned as a watercourse. This flow of water was later contained within a concrete pipe that was laid along the bed of the canal.

Contractors removed the top layers of each of the three locks, scattering the stones and bricks aside. They then filled in the lock chambers, leaving inspection chambers at strategic points. The trust has been working on this site at Tamworth Road since 1998. They have completely rebuilt Lock 25 and work is progressing with Lock 26. The Waterway Recovery Group (WRG), the restoration arm of the Inland Waterways Association, has aided them in this task.

When they started work on Lock 26, there was little to see; simply a gently sloping field that dipped towards the A38. Then WRG moved in and started to clear the soil away. The lock was completely exposed and now the trust's volunteer bricklayers are restoring the structure. Lock 26, like the other two locks, once revealed, has shown that the structure had features of rebuilding by the Birmingham Canal Navigations.

John Horton, engineer for the Lichfield Canal, has investigated all three locks, plus two others, Nos 8 and 30, and noted their make-up. The locks as originally built were constructed with 'orange' bricks, which presumably were made from local clays. The subsequent rebuilding by the BCN replaced only the surface layer, working down from the top towards water level. The amount of reconstruction varied from lock to lock. John has published the following description: 'All locks are of brick construction with single top and double bottom gates. Levels taken at the above locks and other intermediate points show that each lock has a similar drop averaging about 8 feet 10 inches. They were originally constructed of orange coloured, two and a half inch thick, bricks, and the walls were capped by continuous copingstones, typically 8 feet long of local sandstone. The invert was paved in brick and concave, and this paving extended out beyond the bottom gates to protect against scouring. Water entered via drop shafts on both sides with wooden paddles running in cast iron frames and ground posts above. A substantial cast iron striker plate was located at the head of the lock with the water inlet immediately below it, which was connected to the drop shafts by horizontal passages. Water left the chambers via paddles in both bottom gates. Weir passages were of brick except for Lock 26 where it is an open channel.'

The walls at Lock 26 are therefore a mixture of old orange bricks and newer blue engineering bricks. The lock gates comprised two mitred bottom gates and an upper single gate. The construction of the lock has not been altered and this arrangement was evidently used from the start. Stone was used to edge the top of the lock walls and form the quoin stone column for lock gates. This stone appears to have been quarried from the local quarry at Borrowcop Hill and brought to a wharf below Lock 24.

The bottom mitre gates were provided with gate paddles, while there were ground paddles for the upper gates. These ground paddles were contemporary with the lock construction. The paddle gear for the ground paddle was not arranged vertically, but was arranged at a slight angle from the vertical plane. The paddles slid in front of a square-shaped aperture made from a hard, white stone which was not local to the area.

Wooden rubbing boards were originally provided for the locks, but cast iron rubbing beams replaced these in BCN days. When viewed from the waterway, these beams are shown to run along the face of the wing walls at the entrance to the locks and are slightly raised from the brick surface. They are extended through the wall as a thick iron 'tongue'. Bolts through the brickwork pierce this tongue at intervals to provide added strength.

The locks were provided with an overflow weir and channel that diverted water from the upper pound to the lower, while the lock gates were closed. This channel was placed on the offside to the towpath, except at Lock 24. Here the channel was made on the towpath side. The circular weir for this structure was excavated some ten years ago.

Restoration has concentrated on Borrowcop, and Locks 25 and 26 in particular. A new circular weir was installed at Lock 25 and a standard bypass weir at Lock 26. During September 2012, excavation was underway for a new staircase pair of locks near Darnford.

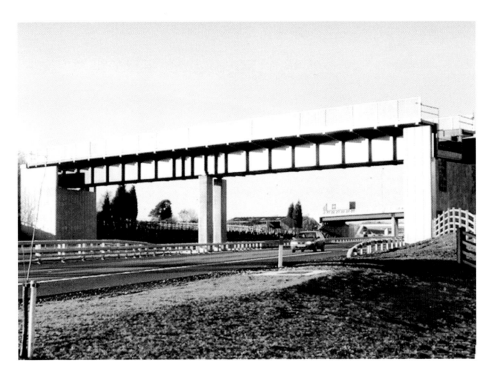

## M6 Toll Aqueduct in Place and Once Toll-Road Opened

The aqueduct was constructed during the period the M6 Toll was being made. The work involved the supply of a new steel aqueduct (supplied by Rowecord Ltd) and the building of concrete support piers. Part of the cost was raised by public subscription (David Suchet Appeal and a donation by the Manifold Trust). John Horton, engineer for LHCT was also involved in getting this project completed. The work was carried out during 2003 with the aqueduct finished and in place in August 2003. The alterations mean that the old Lock 8 will be buried under the west side approach embankment and a new Lock 8 will be made on the east side. (*Photographs: Lichfield & Hatherton Canal Trust*)

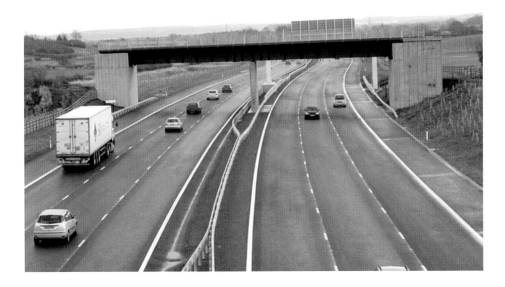

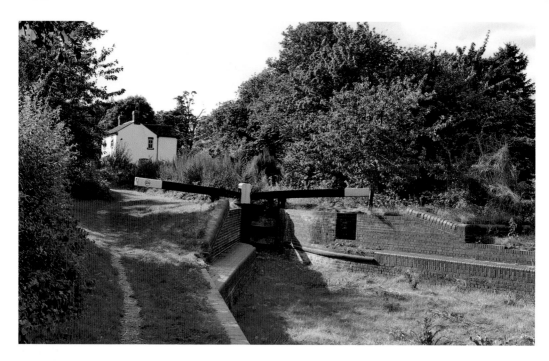

## Lock 24, Lichfield & Circular Weir, Lock 25

(*Above*) The restoration of the canal alongside the A51 at Tamworth Road has been conducted over the last ten years and has led to the complete excavation of lock chambers 25 and 26 and the pounds between Locks 24–27. The set of temporary gates and the canal cottage behind has recreated a canal feature that has been lost for some sixty years. (*Below*) A new feature of the restored lock is a circular weir. This weir was completed in 2010.

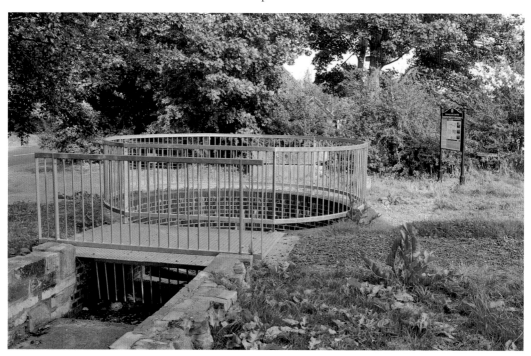

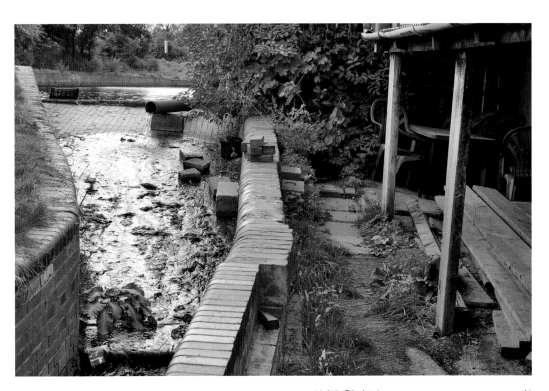

**Weir Lock 26 and LHCT Workshop & Proposals for Locks 27 and 28**
(*Above*) The pound between Locks 25 and 26 has been filled with water. (*Right*) The canal is planned to pass under the A51 in a tunnel, descend through a staircase pair of locks and then continue through a second tunnel under the A38 to join up with the Darnford Lane section.

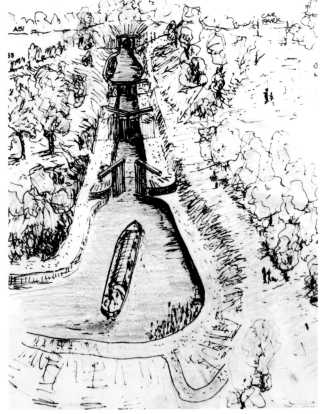

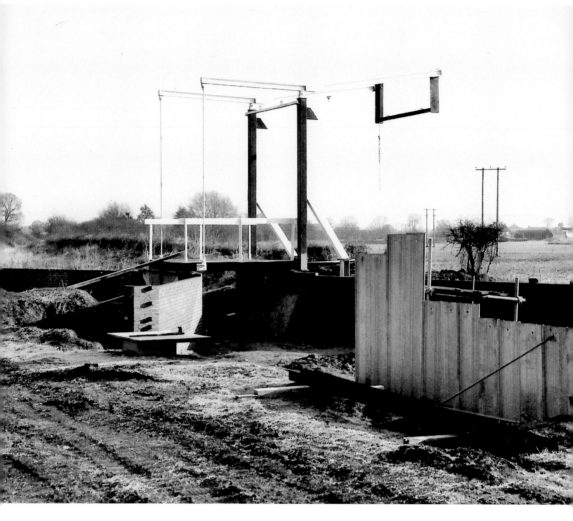

**Lift Bridge Darnford Lane, 1998**
A lift bridge was installed over part of a restored section of the canal near Darnford Lane. Here the route will deviate from the original course to pass through a new Lock 29 and join up with the section presently under restoration.